GOD'S VIBES MATTER

Co-Laboring with God

JULIANA PAGE

BALBOA
PRESS
A DIVISION OF HAY HOUSE

Copyright © 2018 Juliana Page.

All rights reserved. No part of this book may be used or reproduced by any means, graphic, electronic, or mechanical, including photocopying, recording, taping or by any information storage retrieval system without the written permission of the author except in the case of brief quotations embodied in critical articles and reviews.

Bible Scriptures: KJV, NKJV, ESV

Balboa Press books may be ordered through booksellers or by contacting:

Balboa Press
A Division of Hay House
1663 Liberty Drive
Bloomington, IN 47403
www.balboapress.com
1 (877) 407-4847

Because of the dynamic nature of the Internet, any web addresses or links contained in this book may have changed since publication and may no longer be valid. The views expressed in this work are solely those of the author and do not necessarily reflect the views of the publisher, and the publisher hereby disclaims any responsibility for them.

The author of this book does not dispense medical advice or prescribe the use of any technique as a form of treatment for physical, emotional, or medical problems without the advice of a physician, either directly or indirectly. The intent of the author is only to offer information of a general nature to help you in your quest for emotional and spiritual well-being. In the event you use any of the information in this book for yourself, which is your constitutional right, the author and the publisher assume no responsibility for your actions.

Any people depicted in stock imagery provided by Getty Images are models, and such images are being used for illustrative purposes only. Certain stock imagery © Getty Images.

Print information available on the last page.

ISBN: 978-1-9822-0647-5 (sc)
ISBN: 978-1-9822-0649-9 (hc)
ISBN: 978-1-9822-0648-2 (e)

Library of Congress Control Number: 2018906973

Balboa Press rev. date: 06/19/2018

Acknowledgments

I express my deepest appreciation to my family, friends, mentors, and spiritual running buddies; I count it an honor and a privilege to share and do life with you.

To those who continue to fan my flame and encourage me to remain settled in truth, thank you. To those who have gone before me, stewarded mighty mantles, and passed the baton, thank you. To my soulmates who courageously show up to be my mirrors and push me into private discipline and unshakeable trust with the Lord, thank you.

To my partner in purpose for helping me get my fight back and flooding my world with unconditional love, thank you.

For those who have dreamed with me, offered me support and prayers, and infused creativity and care into every labor of love alongside me—you are blessings; thank you.

To all those who rise up and bravely respond to the call of God, thank you.

Contents

Introduction ix
Chapter 1   Heart Check 1
Chapter 2   The Call 30
Chapter 3   The Fight 56
Chapter 4   Divine Assignments 82
Chapter 5   Divine Work 94
Chapter 6   Divine Finances 104
Chapter 7   Divine Family 112
Chapter 8   Divine Relationships 121
Chapter 9   Divine Health 139
Chapter 10 Divine Growth 147
Chapter 11 Divine Elevation 159
Conclusion 168

Introduction

I keep asking that the God of our Lord Jesus Christ, the glorious Father, may give you the Spirit of wisdom and revelation, so that you may know him better. I pray that the eyes of your heart may be enlightened in order that you may know the hope to which he has called you, the riches of his glorious inheritance in his holy people, and his incomparably great power for us who believe.
—Ephesians 1:17–23 (NIV)

The apostle Paul's prayer for the Ephesians still resonates today. If we are living and breathing, we are the generation responsible for establishing ourselves in present truth, steward our unique portions, and walk circumspectly for the benefit of many.

Although our lives can't affect everyone, they can influence those we encounter. It's time that those who have been ignored and oppressed come forth. It's time that those who have been in despair receive encouragement. Many of us have been in the dark, but it is time we hear the voice of the Lord for ourselves and know our true callings.

We would be wise to heed this admonition: "But everything exposed by the light becomes visible—and everything that is illuminated becomes a light." This is why it is said,

> Wake up, sleeper, rise from the dead, and Christ will shine on you. So be very careful how you live—not as unwise but as wise and making the most of every opportunity because the days are evil. Therefore do not be foolish, but understand what the Lord's will is. Do not get drunk on wine, which leads to debauchery. Instead, be filled with the Spirit. (Eph. 5:13–18 NIV)

That is discipleship, but who of us can live with such grace without the conviction and power of God's Holy Spirit? Where will the next generation be if we do not?

Only God can convict and move in our spirits so we experience a change in our hearts that causes us to believe and do supernatural things. No amount of self-help or encouragement can produce what the Holy Spirit alone can. After co-laboring with God to pen *God's Vibes Matter: Reclaiming Your Spiritual Authority*, I realized how God's love would communicate to those who have their spiritual senses exercised to discern his presence.

Jesus is God's ultimate revealer. He is continually internally speaking to humankind, and he desires free-flowing communication. God sent us the Bible so we could hear his mind, will, and heart. This life has never been about our agenda and ministry; it's about his kingdom and glory. Depending on our upbringing and experience in addition to our exposure or lack of it to the Word of God, we may feel that God has forgotten us or has sidelined us, but that couldn't be further from the truth. For this reason, it is important to know our identity in Christ and the authority this brings to our lives. What's most important is personally and regularly communicating with God; that will enhance a quality relationship and walk with Christ by increasing the ability to talk with God and hear what he says.

God requires his people to be open to and mature in their walk. The enemy wants us to walk in darkness, but God stirs us up when we are in darkness.

> Arise, shine, for your light has come, and the glory of the Lord rises upon you. See, darkness covers the earth and thick darkness is over the peoples, but the Lord rises upon you and his glory appears over you. Nations will come to your light, and kings to the brightness of your dawn. (Isa. 60:1–3 NIV)

Does this not stir something up in your soul? It is a promise of future glory.

Our spirits are activated through divine encounters with God's Word and the Holy Spirit, which produces freedom and personal evangelism on a mass scale. We receive a spirit of wisdom and revelation so we can know God better and learn all he has for believers.

If this generation needs anything, it is an increase of faith. This book is an opportunity for believers to become sensitive to the voice of the Holy Spirit, to become the "stirring up" of the faith in the acts they do, and to become consistent demonstrations of Christ as enabled by the Holy Spirit in all they do.

Living in and for the glory of the Lord is a partnership with Christ, a co-laboring that provides the strength to live a life of integrity that glorifies God. On our own, apart from God, this life is impossible, but,

> Now the Lord is the Spirit, and where the Spirit of the Lord is, there is freedom. And we all, who with unveiled faces contemplate the Lord's glory, are being transformed into his image with ever-increasing glory, which comes from the Lord, who is the Spirit. (2 Cor. 3:17–18 NIV)

Did you catch that? The presence of the Holy Spirit, the same Spirit who was in Jesus, can live in us, and accepting him can give us freedom from fear, guilt, sin, and oppression. The Holy Spirit is our hope and life-giving energy that manifests as we turn from unbelief and waywardness as a quickening in our spirits. This quickening brings enlightenment, renewed minds, and when that happens, we will be in the presence of the Holy Spirit, encounter the Lord's glory, and grow in our understanding of him and his divine attributes—wisdom, power, goodness, truth, justice, mercy, holiness, and grace. If this generation walks in this kind of love, what a movement that will be. Are you inspired to be a part of that?

It occurred to me while in a mentoring session with my sweet, fifteen-year-old mentee that our youth have a deep hunger for and need of strong spiritual leadership. I was moved to reflect on how this young woman absorbed wisdom and godly counsel so freely from our relationship. At her age, I didn't know how to ask for or receive that kind of encouragement.

Her mother told me how her daughter had been benefitting from our connection and how she'd recently scored her best yet on an article she wrote for school about our meetings. The mother began to cry and said, "You're changing her life." How powerful and reassuring a word like that can be when you need it most. I had been fearful, intimidated, and restless as a fifteen-year-old, but that was not going to be my mentee's story.

Ralph Waldo Emerson said, "To know even one life has breathed easier because you have lived. This is to have succeeded." What if we lived under the reality of these words? I'd almost given up the opportunity to mentor because of my schedule, but God made me remember that when my mentee's mother thanked me for my influence in her daughter's life. I was humbled and grateful God had allowed this mentorship to impact me as much as it had my mentee.

To think that we live to ourselves is one of the biggest lies. The apostle Paul encouraged his mentee: "For this reason I remind you to fan into flame the gift of God, which is in you through the laying on of my hands. For the Spirit God gave us does not make us timid, but gives us power, love and self-discipline" (2 Tim. 1:6–7 NIV). The laying on of hands releases a gift of God. We can have a gift, but we must release it, in this case by the laying on of hands. The encouragement from Paul was that something supernatural happened when we invested in, prayed for, and laid hands on people. There is literally a spirit change because God did not give anyone a spirit that does not produce power, love, or self-control, which we receive when the Holy Spirit comes upon us. Why would Paul need to remind Timothy to remember to fan into flames the gift of God, the Holy Spirit? Perhaps it was because people do not always live in this reality.

If we look at this iceberg image, we see that much of what is physically seen, what we reveal to that world, does not reveal the depth of what we are dealing with inside.

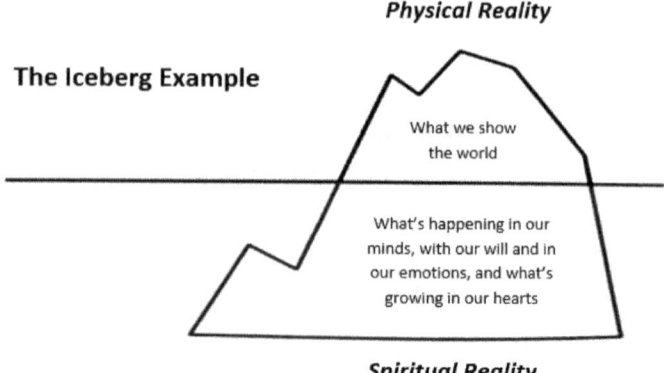

This image shows we have a significantly different reality hidden in Christ, a reality that can be seen only in the physical world if we are constantly in partnership with God and stirring up his faith in us.

This also gives us insight into God's reality. If God did not give us a spirit of fear and we were not born with fear, that means we've learned our fears. We pick up different fears, and even more than learning them, we believe them. We will demonstrate above the surface whatever we believe below the surface. If we believe the lie that we can't speak in public, we'll avoid doing so at all costs. If we believe the lie that we can't fly safely in an airplane, we won't travel. If we believe the lie that we'll fail at something, we won't risk doing it.

But if we've learned to fear, we can unlearn to fear. We can replace every lie we've learned with the truth of God's Word. Can you imagine that? What would this generation be if it were stirred up in faith and set free of fear and intimidation? Do you believe the Holy Spirit can set you free?

We currently live in a culture of fear and panic. It is rare that we can turn on the news or pull up our social media pages and hear good news. We're in a culture in which fear sells.

The Bible says a sign of the times is that the people would be tempted to fear, "But make up your mind not to worry beforehand how you will defend yourselves" (Luke 21:14 NIV). Fear is a physical reality all around us; it is a spirit trying to intimidate us. We live in fear of war, disease, and natural disasters. This generation is under attack by fear as we've never seen before. This is not God's will or plan as we've read in Ephesians but quite the opposite. This kind of spiritual attack will not be countered just by positive thinking.

If we are afraid, we're usually in the world but not making a real impact on it. It's almost as if we're repeating history and playing it safe rather than making history. Fear puts us in the game, but we don't make an impact. Fear allows us to exist but not live—not thrive but simply survive. Fear makes us a part of culture but not a counterculture. Is a safe and comfortable life a good life?

One thing is for sure—the enemy wants us to be timid; he knows he can't stop us, so he just tries to intimidate us and slow us down in anything we're after. The spirit of fear wants us to hang our heads, feel powerless, and always believe the worst will happen. Maybe then, it's not so much about us feeling forgotten by God but us failing to remember him and seek him with all we have.

I'll give you an illustration of the spirit of fear. I'm not originally from Texas, but one of the most fascinating things I've witnessed there was longhorns. My mother has a best friend who raises longhorn cattle. I'm from the Midwest and have seen tons of cows in my day, but longhorns were something else. The way they walked with their heads low and dragging their horns on the ground caught my interest. I learned that was normal due to the weight of their horns, which increased in time. It would get to the point that they could not lift their heads. That sounds like how the enemy subtly uses fear to become our normal way of operating, and we bow our heads.

Have you found yourself walking with your head low because it was weighed down by old thoughts, old relationships, old names that you've agreed with, and old environments? That is not needed or necessary for where you're headed. Leviticus tells us it's quite the opposite: "I am the LORD your God, who brought you out of the land of Egypt so you would no longer be their slaves. I broke the yoke of slavery from your neck so you can walk with your heads held high" (Lev. 26:13 NLT).

This is your new posture—you are confident and bold with your head held high. You need to know that all your needs have been met and that if you've turned your life over to Jesus, he's already broken the chains of your past and your slavery to your mistakes so you can walk with your head held high: "It is for freedom that Christ has set us free. Stand firm, then, and do not let yourselves be burdened again by a yoke of slavery" (Gal. 5:1 NIV).

This is important to note right at the jump because you must have made up your mind to not live under, return to, or continue to live in the yoke of slavery. In this book, you'll come across things that apply to your life where you are walking with you head held low, but knowing God's call on your life and working in his Word will make all the difference. But you cannot do that if you've accepted slavery rather than freedom.

You can make an incredible impact in the life God has already planned for you, but that requires that you break out of intimidation, break through the crowd, and step out by faith. If you step out, God will meet you.

The Holy Spirit did something amazing for me in 2015, and I believe he'll do the same for you. He set me free from the spirit of intimidation and drew my attention to the strategy he'd given the apostle Paul: "One night the Lord spoke to Paul in a vision: 'Do not be afraid; keep on speaking, do not be silent'" (Acts 18:9 NIV). This was prophetic and profound. The apostle Paul never spoke about the fears he encountered, but it was obvious he battled fear because God told him not to be afraid.

I realized that though I too had tried my humble best to remain calm, cool, and collected amid many of my challenging life experiences, I could not deny the spiritual cancer in me that was trying to destroy me. That brought conviction to my spirit. How can you not be afraid when you have all that going on beneath the surface? God's approach with Paul was interesting. He didn't condemn Paul for being afraid; he told him not to be afraid and gave him a strategy to break the fear—keep talking.

I learned that that talk would become my spiritual edge. My old, unrenewed nature, my shy, quiet, and reserved self became transformed after hearing God's Word and speaking it with all I had because I was sick and tired of feeling sick and tired. I started praying at a level that probably made my neighbors wonder what I was doing in my home and fellow motorists wonder what I was doing in my car; they must have thought I was on my Bluetooth screaming at someone. They didn't know I was miraculously praying and with some attitude. I was speaking with an anointing of the Holy Spirit, and I refused to be silent.

Yes, it initially felt uncomfortable, and I thought I was going a little crazy, but I was willing to do that to break my bonds that had had me in a stranglehold for years. I declared the promises of God and did not stop because I knew that speaking God's Word and praising his name was the antidote to fear.

Fear lurking beneath the surface of our physical reality is not dispelled just by thinking your way out of it. Fear is on the inside, but it's broken on the outside. A battle is going on in your mind, but you win it by speaking and declaring the Word of God.

Fear is a liar, and after fear lies to you, it paralyzes you. That's why a silent soul is a dying soul. Fear will stop more people than failure ever will. Therefore, we are called to wake up and stir up faith rather than fear in our souls. When we don't know how to worship or pray, we unconsciously trade in our peace for restlessness and intimidation. If we are not talking, we are letting the internal battle get the best of us. But God tells us not to be afraid. We've been given full permission to be bold with faith—to sing, praise, celebrate, and declare God's promises over our lives for the sake of our lives. If we are, whatever is attacking us inside will be broken.

This book is your invitation to know the hope God has called you to, and it gives you confidence to say, "I'm chosen for this!" This book offers revelation words of his glorious inheritance for you—an anticipation and acceptance that God wants to get his goodness to you more than you do. It also offers divine encounters and real manifestations of his power—an awareness that God reveals himself personally to you and you can believe what he tells you to the degree that you rest and declare, "It is so! Thank you, God!"

This book is a process of refinement; if we allow God to free us from our sins and burdens, we will walk clean before the Lord and fulfill our calls. By the grace of God, we can cast off fear and put on the faith of God that brings light that dispels darkness.

If you choose faith, you choose to believe something good will happen. Here are four things I believe this generation will shake off and get free from if they choose faith.

1. Fear of others. Some of us are so afraid of what people think of us that we expend all our creative energy maintaining an image. Here's what Proverbs says: "Fear of man will prove to be a snare, but whoever trusts in the Lord is kept safe" (Prov. 29:25 NIV).

   When we fear others, we watch them live their lives at the expense of our own. When we look and compare, we don't move forward or back; we're just stuck. If we allow fear of others to control us, we will be stuck and forsake our destinies.

   God wants this generation to be free of worrying about what others think about us. Others' opinion of us is none of our business. God wants us to live for him, an audience of one. We can live with a Holy Spirit confidence that loves others but that also knows God's call and keeps moving forward despite others' thoughts and opinions.

2. Fear of the future. Aye, future tripping as I like to say. It's easy to be convinced that the world is just getting darker and darker so why even try to serve, to make an impact, or to have influence and help?

   But God says something very different about the future: "'For I know that plans I have for you,' declares the LORD, 'plans to prosper you and not to harm you, plans to give you hope and a future'" (Jer. 29:11 NIV). Jesus wants us looking forward with hope and confidence that he's secured good futures for us.

   Though we don't know what the future holds, we have been divinely instructed not to fear it. If God holds the future and he is in our future, a place has been prepared for us. David said it like this: "I had fainted, unless I had believed to see the goodness of the LORD in the land of the living" (Ps. 27:13 KJV).

Just because something hasn't worked doesn't mean it will never work. We can press on in the hope of witnessing God's goodness. There will be better days, better relationships, and better opportunities for us. We should not doubt that God is in our future and preparing it.

3. Fear of failure. This sounds like, "What if it doesn't work? What if I pray but don't get an answer? What if I try that business and it doesn't succeed?" Failure is not failure, but this is why mind-sets can be failures. Failure is good for you because it humbles you. Even if something doesn't turn out the way you expected, at least you can say you learned something and rest knowing that you're not wondering what could have or should have happened.

   We can be better for whatever we've attempted and achieved. Every attempt to obey God honors him. Just attempting to demonstrate our faith honors his heart. We don't need to wait on a perfect situation to step out; we can step out and find out. We'll figure out our success as we co-labor with God.

4. Fear of the enemy. We don't have to fear a defeated foe; Jesus conquered our enemy on the cross and told us, "I have given you authority to trample on snakes and scorpions and to overcome all the power of the enemy; nothing will harm you" (Luke 10:19 NIV). This means we don't have to fear what seems to form against us.

The blessing of being a child of God is that if God is for you, nothing can harm you.

Fear is not something you have to cope with; God has created you to conquer fear. When the light of God is on you, you don't have to fear the darkness. Timothy was afraid. He was a young pastor who had experienced explosive growth in his ministry but wasn't sure how to lead himself, the church, and the elders. Timothy was right in the will of God but was intimidated.

Paul reminded Timothy to look back and see God's faithfulness throughout his life. He reminded him of the divine encounter they'd had where the Holy Spirit came upon him and he began to prophecy. He reminded him to never stop speaking God's Word. Paul told Timothy exactly what Jesus had told him. You don't have to live with intimidation or fear; you just keep declaring what God said and you will experience a breakthrough.

When Jesus sets you free and you walk it out, you can live in freedom. God said,

> You are the light of the world. A town built on a hill cannot be hidden. Neither do people light a lamp and put it under a bowl. Instead they put it on its stand, and it gives light to everyone in the house. In the same way, let your light shine before others, that they may see your good deeds and glorify your Father in heaven. (Matt. 5:14–16 NIV)

This is what you can have strongly rooted beneath the surface. This can be your reality, but it requires coming out of the fog of fear, obligation, and guilt. God has a different fog for you—the fire, oil, and glorious anointing of his Holy Spirit. Will you challenge yourself with the truth so you can rise in faith and receive the grace to do what the Bible says you can do?

I hope this book will activate your yes life, your willingness to keep saying yes to God and learning more about his life-giving truth that will help you experience and steward this freedom in your life. Maybe what you thought would bring happiness has not proven to be true.

Worldly Happiness	Holy Spirit Grace
universe	Jesus
energy	Holy Spirit flow
positive feelings	peace
ease	grace
synchronicity	anointing
déjà vu	presence
luck	blessing
achievement	destiny
accomplishment	legacy
mystical	favor
recognition	impact

Happiness is an inside job, a heart issue. The worst lies you will ever believe are those you tell yourself. Jesus said, "Do not suppose that I have come to bring peace to earth. I did not come to bring peace, but a sword" (Matt. 10:34 NIV). He came to bring a sword against the fog of the enemy. An unrenewed mind can't know God's will or what can bring it true joy. Joy is contentment, and I have it because I've been tested so many times that I finally surrendered and decided to believe the best and not think the worst.

I've decided to walk by faith and trust God with what I don't understand. I don't know how things will turn out most of the time, but I believe God. It's a choice. This didn't happen suddenly for me; after I really suffered and went through a lot, I made up my mind that I'd let nothing steal my joy and that I'd accomplish what God had called me to do. I prioritize God and do what he tells me to do. I'm not led by how I feel. I want God to trust and use me, but he can't if my thoughts are negative and selfish. I am working my way out of that old bondage by the Word of God.

When I committed to co-laboring with God, he showed me how an old coaching tool I'd once utilized could be repurposed to more clearly see if I was keeping Jesus front and center in my life. He said, "Seek ye first the kingdom of God, and his righteousness; and all these things shall be added unto you" (Matt. 6:33 NIV). This verse is the divine strategy for keeping Jesus at the center of all you do. You'll see in this image my old way, my unrenewed way of living was to consider and dream up all I wanted for my life—my agenda, preferences, desires, and opinions. But my controlled wheel of life led to unhappiness.

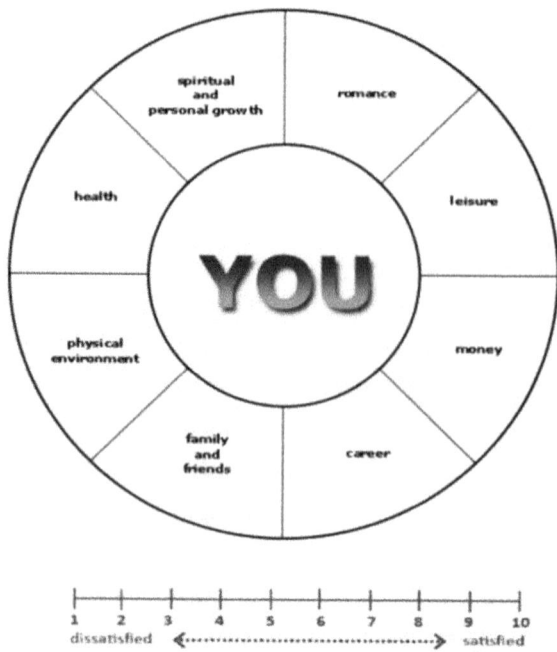

The Old, Unrenewed You

The focus of the wheel is you, and you filter categories or different areas of your life. The aim of the wheel-of-life exercise is to look at each life area and determine how satisfied you are with it on a scale of 1 to 10. A 10 means you're completely satisfied with that area and don't see any need to change what's in it.

As you rate each area, you will quickly determine what areas are weak versus what areas are strong and where you have the greatest need and opportunity for improvement. This image reflects an unrenewed you, meaning you would likely come up with your own strategies or hire a coach to help you come up with strategies to increase your levels of satisfaction. For example, maybe you give a 4 to the money area of your life. You or your coach would assess why you rated that area a 4 and brainstorm about what would help move that number toward

10. Your strategies could involve creating a budget, building an investment portfolio, or saving more. After you decide on the best strategy, you come up with an accountability plan and timeline. While this is a great exercise and self-help assessment tool, it can also reveal how spiritually off center your life is.

Because I was misguided about what my true source of power was, where it came from, and what I was supposed to do with it, I became tired of reinventing myself as life demanded. I wanted to really know my identity and unique calling I was here to fulfill and get on with it. Anyone else?

Someone said, "People of vision see the invisible, hear the inaudible, think the unthinkable, believe the incredible, and do the impossible." I agree with that, but what if your vision doesn't align with God's vision for your life? What if God is not who you are hearing and collaborating with? You could miss the call on your life, and you could become distracted and forfeit it.

We see this in the book of Esther, where her cousin and guardian Mordecai encouraged her to face her fears for the sake of her community.

> For if you remain silent now, relief and deliverance for the Jews will arise from another place, but you and your father's family will perish. And who knows but that you have come to your royal position for such a time as this? (Est. 4:14 NIV)

Mordecai told Esther that she could forfeit the opportunity but that even if she did, God would bring out his divine will through another source. Would you want to miss out on what

God had planned for you? Let us delight in discovering his call and will for us.

The Bible says, "To each is given the manifestation of the Spirit for the common good" (1 Cor. 12:7 ESV). God is raising men and women of character. If you are in a place of transition, he is likely getting your character and integrity in place for what he's about to do. It can be uncomfortable as God works to rid you of your insecurity, pride, fear, and anxiety, but once he does, you will readily step out on what God has called you to do.

We can co-labor with the Holy Spirit and appropriate the full power and authority Christ set aside for us. It's one thing to have vision, but each of us must have a personal revelation that Jesus has called, equipped, and enabled us to manifest his supernatural life and power through our lives.

This perspective inspires us to persevere through the pruning and preparation process until we are equipped to reach our divine mandates. Maybe this image speaks to you.

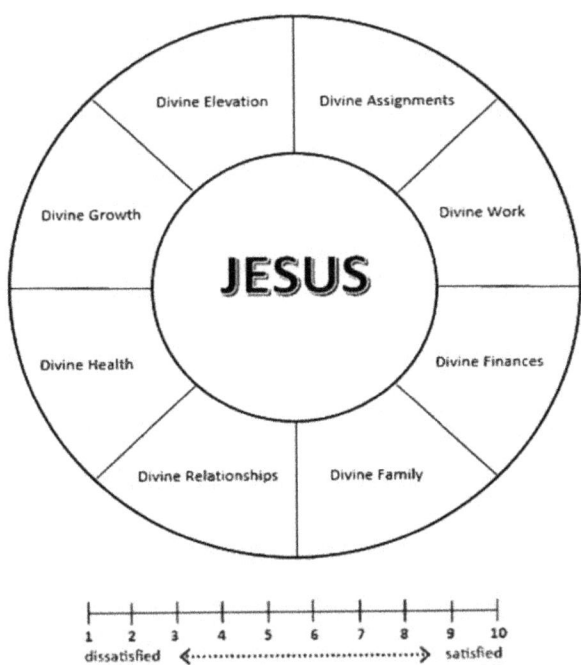

The New Creation of You

In this image, Jesus is in the center and is the filter for all your life areas. Each area on the wheel is divinely inspired and orchestrated. In this setup, the satisfaction rating as a new creation is still 1 through 10, but that's determined by how satisfied you are with yielding to and obeying the Holy Spirit's guidance.

If you give the money area a 4 here, you would then connect with your coach, Jesus, and allow the Holy Spirit to speak to you regarding why you rated that area a 4. You may receive conviction about paying your tithes or maybe a revelation about a limiting belief you have about finances that God didn't plant in your heart; it could still be rooted and active there holding you back from feeling it's a 10, the abundance he has for you in that area.

Through this exercise, you can clearly assess your discipleship.

> You are the salt of the earth; but if the salt has lost its taste (purpose), how can it be made salty? It is no longer good for anything, but to be thrown out and walked on by people [when the walkways are wet and slippery]. (Matt. 5:13–16 AMP)

You can determine if you have lost your saltiness in other areas as well or where others may not be able to see your good deeds and moral excellence. That will let you make adjustments as inspired and enabled by the Holy Spirit. This is a "by grace through faith" process: "For it is by grace you have been saved, through faith—and this is not from yourselves, it is the gift of God—not by works, so that no one can boast" (Eph. 2:8–9 NIV).

God can work with you to make changes in your life: "You will receive power when the Holy Spirit comes on you" (Acts 1:8 NIV); you can do all God requires of you. You can co-labor with God when you allow the Holy Spirit to renew your thoughts and take on a new nature; instead of waking up and reading social media, you will want to read the Bible and renew your mind concerning the areas you're struggling with.

This is your armor against the attacks of darkness. This is what you must fight with, and God will always guide you when you ask him to. As God's salt and light, you can choose daily to stir yourself up in the Lord and prevent old thoughts and unrenewed attributes from blurring your light walk. You will have an impact and be an example in every dark place rather than be infected by every dark place.

Is this you?	Do you need this?
Hunger for closeness with God	Personal consecration
Feel desire for a fresh anointing	Kill murmuring and complaining
Desperate for a new season	Hear God clearly; know his purpose and will for your life
Don't want to carry old things forward	Take better care of your temple—eat better, move your body, and increase your prayer life
Want to make sure you shake off any unhealthy habits or connections	Financial, relational, or career breakthroughs
Want to function with confidence and excellence	Tailor-made blessings and expansion
Want to be armed and guard against attack	Open doors and divine alignments
Want to create a new normal	Step into next level

If this is you, here is what God is saying: "Come to me continually in every circumstance you confront and our continued fellowship will make you victorious. My power can flow through your prayers to me. Discipline in life will enable you to have a close relationship with me. Strong, calm sanity comes from being intimate with me. Bring me your firstfruits. Partner with me in all you do and you will not be put to shame."

Contentment comes from giving dynamic, tension-giving, appropriate attention to all areas of your life. God, your filter, will help you stay focused on what matters most. Prioritize and organize your life around him. Let God manage your opportunities while you focus on being rightly related to him.

You need to know where you are and strive for all God has promised you can be. Picture each area as he spoke it to be. Use your imagination to see what God sees.

Each chapter of this book represent a different area of your life. As you rate each area to determine how much you're co-laboring with God and surrender each area to God, your understanding of how you can adapt to each area and embrace God's will for you will increase.

The antidote to your unrest is complete trust in God. He invites you to get out of living by your power alone and instead pursue God as your joy dealer. As you begin to discover his heart, which enables you to be content, you will feed your spirit and delight in the good news he has for you. If you could use something to help you prepare for your life, would you do the work? God will show you how. Sit at his feet and let him pour wisdom into you. Yield to God and what he wants to do with you. Renew your mind so you will receive what your heart needs and not be deceived.

God gives you authority to bring his will to earth, not to bring your will to pass. It's time to say no to deception, reject the lies, and walk in freedom. When you choose to give God your yes and get free, you will move in purpose and change the world. Go through a consecrated season, die to yourself, get put back together, and relearn yourself in God filled with his wisdom and strength. Intentionally prepare, get your soul healed, learn who you are, establish wholeness, and pour it into others.

Jesus can be the holding power in your life. Don't let anything or anyone cause you to not have intimacy with him. It is only in picking up your cross—losing your lower life—that you are worthy of God and his higher life: "We are therefore Christ's ambassadors, as though God were making his appeal through us. We implore you on Christ's behalf: Be reconciled to God" (2 Cor. 5:20 NIV).

Chapter 1

Heart Check

> Restore to me the joy of your salvation and
> grant me a willing spirit, to sustain me.
> —Psalm 51:12 (NIV)

Have you ever wondered what God requires of you? It seems like a silly question, but it's one worth digging into especially if we are instructed to "love the Lord your God will all your heart, and with all your soul, and with all your strength, and with all your mind; and love your neighbor as yourself" (Luke 10:27 NIV). This weighty verse covers so many of the others. Imagine if we could get this one rooted in us. We can't love God well if we don't know him or what he requires. If we could focus on what God requires, we'd see what his love looks like and be equipped to share it.

"He has shown you, O mortal, what is good. And what does the LORD require of you? To act justly and to love mercy and to walk humbly with your God" (Mic. 6:8 NIV). Let's break down the Lord's requirements.

ACT JUSTLY

The power and authority Christ gives us is never for evil but for good. As ambassadors for Christ, we are to treat people fairly and focus on what will build one another up, not taking advantage of the weak, not forgetting or overlooking people who helped us, not betraying friends, not controlling or using others for personal gain, and not destroying people through slander.

LOVE MERCY

We are to do our best to model compassion to ourselves and others by being forgiving and kind, helping the oppressed, and blessing those who curse us. We can decide not to live in critical, self-righteous, or condemning attitudes and behaviors.

WALK HUMBLY

It takes genuine humility to have faith. We can't readily depend on God if we're vain, proud, rude, selfish, or arrogant. Humility means not looking down on others and not engaging in self-promotion. Humility is a willingness to always be teachable, being willing to receive correction, and not thinking of ourselves more highly than we ought. The humble are quick to admit it and apologize when they're wrong.

We don't have space in our souls and we haven't been given the responsibility to judge ourselves or others. We are designed to be just, love kindness, and walk humbly with our God because that brings us freedom and allows our witness to glorify God.

We've also been given an antidote cocktail of power, love, and self-discipline to live above fear: "For the Spirit God gave us does not make us timid, but gives us power, love and self-discipline" (2 Tim. 1:7 NIV). It takes knowing what God requires of us and his Holy Spirit to obey him.

David in the Psalms truly had a heart after God. Numerous times, David cried out to the Lord, "Give me again the joy that comes from your salvation, and make me willing to obey you" (Ps. 51:12 GNT). "Search me, God, and know my heart; test me and know my anxious thoughts. See if there is any offensive way in me, and lead me in the way everlasting" (Ps. 139:23–24 NIV).

The heart question asks, is my life pointing others to God? If God were to take a tuning fork and ring it against my soul, would our rhythms match? If Christlikeness is our effect as ambassadors, I believe we are being called to divine encounters. We can meet with God, hear his voice, delight in his Word, and grow in revelatory knowledge of him in these encounters. We can learn the unforced rhythms of grace through divine encounters. Matthew says it like this.

> Are you tired? Worn out? Burned out on religion? Come to me. Get away with me and you'll recover your life. I'll show you how to take a real rest. Walk with me and work with me—watch how I do it. Learn the unforced rhythms of grace. I won't lay anything heavy or ill-fitting on you. Keep company with me and you'll learn to live freely and lightly. (Matt. 11:28–30 MSG)

Divine encounters allow God to rightly divide and tune us, and we get holy, most excellent faith so we can stir up our call. Divine encounters matter immensely because consecrating ourselves in a world that is frustrated, in an identity crisis, and scattered by insecurities demands that we be serious about living with power, love, and self-control. Our consecration is an inner security the enemy will do everything he can to prevent us from having.

Have you ever had the gnawing feeling that you weren't getting everything you were supposed to get out of life? A feeling that life was full of possibilities but somehow you could never figure out how to tap into them?

Frustration comes from living a life apart from God—a life in which he is not consistently present in our thoughts and words. God wired our thoughts and words to have power so we'd be equipped to overcome every obstacle. Without consistent exposure to the ultimate power source—our light source—our hearts are not hooked up to the provision they need.

Our relationship with God determines who we become in our spirits, so we need to get serious about this "presence" business if we want to experience the joy of our deliverance and have daily sustenance. The Word of God has the power to realign anything that is misaligned especially faulty mind-sets, beliefs, ideologies, traditions, and doctrines that lie and exalt themselves above the will of God for your life.

Life doesn't have to be a frustrating mystery.

> The mystery that has been kept hidden for ages and generations, but is now disclosed to the Lord's people. To them God has chosen to make known among the Gentiles the glorious riches of this mystery, which is Christ in you, the hope of glory. (Col. 1:26–27 NIV)

Christ in us is the hope of glory. God designed us to be hope carriers if we choose. We can learn to take our nourishment from God, get our supply from him, and feed on his Word. If we continually go back to the foundation of our affections and recollect where the source of power is, we may find we rely on God's presence as much as we rely on oxygen. Realizing where our help really comes from makes us stronger.

Christ in us brings hope of all great things to come. He helps us remain poised for the future. If we're willing to be restored and go through the process, we can co-labor with God to restore the years that seemed wasted and redeem the time. Our part is consecrating; his is sanctifying. The problem is that they key to receiving all this is a relationship with God, and the enemy does not want us to know the power and authority we have in Christ.

Faith and fear are opposites, but they are similar in two ways: they are both about the future and they both begin in the mind. This means that if the enemy can seduce us into hardening our hearts, he can keep God from being the ruling authority in our minds and shift the course of our future. God is relational and wants to communicate his desires, plans, and purposes to us. The question is whether we will commit to taking time to grow in this relationship, for he is our God and we are the people of his pasture and the flock under his care. But we must hear him when he says, "Do not harden your hearts as you did at Meribah, as you did that day at Massah in the wilderness" (Ps. 95:7–8 NIV).

In our narcissistic, self-consumed society, many have moved away from the global plan of God for humanity. We tend to focus on what's in it for us. It's not that we haven't been warned, "A person may think their own ways are right, but the LORD weighs the heart" (Prov. 21:2 NIV); rather, we've grown comfortable with mixing fear and faith and drifting from God's presence.

Sometimes, God will provoke us to inspire us to turn our hearts back to him. We see this in Romans, where the Lord provoked Israel with the Gentiles.

> Just as it is written, "God gave them a spirit of stupor, Eyes to see not and ears to hear not, Down to this very day." And David says, "Let their table become a snare and a trap, And a stumbling block and a retribution to them. Let their eyes be darkened to see not, And bend their backs forever." I say then, they did not stumble so as to fall, did they? May it never be! But by their transgression salvation *has come* to the Gentiles, to make them jealous. Now if their transgression is riches for the world and their failure is riches for the Gentiles, how much more will their fulfillment be. (Rom. 11:8–12)

The apostle Paul grappled with helping us understand that God had a plan for a people who for the most part had rejected him. The Gentiles were limited in their experience of God through Jesus, so the church moving into a state of grace or being given the space to enter something happened to provoke Israel.

God sometimes provokes us to move into something that we would otherwise not have moved into. Many of us are where we are today because God used something or someone to provoke us. There is another way we can live life, and there is always a choice. God often uses things to disrupt our lives and provoke us to hunger. This provocation comes through exposure—if you know better, you do better. The exposure to better is to provoke us to change because change never comes easy.

Not everybody is provoked by better. There is also an option to become envious; instead of being provoked to discover their greatness, some become envious. We see this as the case with Hannah and Peninnah in Samuel. God allowed Hannah to see someone who had what she'd desperately wanted to provoke her to wonder, *If God did it for another woman, could he still do it for me?* God wanted Hannah to be provoked because she was barren and she'd decided having a child was not to be for her. She started to believe it was impossible because that was easier than believing for something that didn't seem to be happening, and she didn't want to get her hopes up.

Our carnal nature will make a deal to keep us from being provoked to stretch into the next dimension; it will talk us out of the discomfort of believing God. But God didn't want Hannah to settle into her unbelief: "Because the LORD had closed Hannah's womb, her rival kept provoking her in order to irritate her" (1 Sam. 1:6 NIV). God wanted Hannah stirred up and hungry for more. What happened when Hannah was stirred up?

> In her deep anguish Hannah prayed to the LORD, weeping bitterly. And she made a vow, saying, "LORD Almighty, if you will only look on your servant's misery and remember me, and not forget your servant but give her a son, then I will give him to the LORD for all the days of his life, and no razor will ever be used on his head" (1 Sam. 1:10–11 NIV)

She relentlessly poured out her soul to the Lord.

> And the Lord remembered her. So, in the course of time Hannah became pregnant and gave birth to a son. She named him Samuel, saying, "Because I asked the Lord for him." (1 Sam. 6:20 NLT)

When Hannah was provoked, she decided to repent and turn from all the anger and bitterness she'd stirred up against her rival, Peninnah, and she gave birth in a divine setup. Like Hannah, God will provoke us to want more, to want to be better, to be a more excellent servants, witnesses, and persons. He wants us to know we can be like Hannah. We can trade in our old, worn-out lives for new ones. We can decide to let the better part of us come forth.

But if it were that easy, we'd all be doing it. The truth is, we believe only what we're willing to act on. Look around the world; it seems there are more hearts caught up in unbelief than desiring to hear God's secrets. It's unfortunate because God created us to not know what shame feels like; it renders so many ineffective, and the enemy will always try to shame us in the areas God wants to use us. Where guilt says, "I did something wrong," shame says, "Something's wrong with me." Too often, we see people unaware of or forgetting that God has never disqualified us. If we confess our sins, he will cleanse us of all our unrighteousness. Somewhere, we got stuck and stopped flourishing and thriving in our relationship with Christ.

Fortunately, the truth will set us free, and we can abide in it. When the devil wanted to bring down humanity, he used words, so we see an assault on the Word of God. Too many are having conversations with the enemy rather than speaking and doing what God says and walking in the fullness of his promises. A downhill spiral begins when the enemy's voice is elevated above God's. Live your own way, get your identity from yourself rather than your Creator, amass what you want, and you'll be doing the antithesis of what God wants and living for the devil.

We can live from what we know and stop acting like we came from nothing. Obedience to God helps us flourish in life—it's freedom, not legalism. God knows how we work best. He gave us the keys to abundant living in his Word, but we have to obey it.

So often, we run from God instead of to him, but he always sees us as worthy. The enemy wants to keep us from his presence. Will you decide to get out of hiding? In Genesis, Adam was fearful, ashamed, and hiding from God. "But the LORD God called to the man, 'Where are you?' He answered, 'I heard you in the garden, and I was afraid because I was naked; so I hid'" (Gen. 3:9–10 NIV).

That is where we fell. We started believing lies that stopped us from being propelled toward God and our God-given purpose. We forgot that we were his, that we had everything we needed in him, and that we had no need to minimize the potential we carried. We need a generation of people who come out of hiding, control their environment, and fight what they hear with revelation. We can make what God says bigger than anything else, but we must be hungry for it and committed to fighting the constant lies of the enemy by asking, Did God really say it? Do we know who we are in Christ? Where are you? Where is the you God created? Who told you?

If you want to know where your heart is, look where your mind goes when it wanders. You may not like what you find there. You underestimate how hungry your soul is for real food. You mindlessly feed your mind and therefore your soul so much junk day in and day out. And then when you turn to the good stuff, the God stuff, and turn off the noise, you find yourself at home full, happy, and peaceful again. You have to fight to protect your soul, but that won't be easy.

It's time to divorce what you want so God can give you what he wants for your life. If you decide to follow Jesus, you'll never be the same. Maybe you know about God but don't know God. Maybe you need Jesus. Maybe you realize you can't do whatever you need to do and need God to do it. Maybe you realize that you can't be good enough on your own, that you need the perfect sacrifice of Jesus. Do you need help breaking some agreements by activating new ones?

Place your faith in what Christ did on the cross. Maybe you were tempted, you went through a trial, and for whatever reason you turned your back on God but you want to come back home as the Prodigal Son wanted. If the Holy Spirit is knocking on your heart's door, will you give him a shot? Do you need him? Do you want to know that heaven's your home, that Jesus is your Lord, that your sin has been forgiven, that your past has been wiped away, and that you can become a new creation? Something happens when you move.

If you want to become a new creation, pray this prayer. "Jesus, forgive me. I turn away from my old life, and I turn to you. Make me new; change me from the inside out. I believe Jesus Christ died on a cross, was buried, and rose from the dead. Save me now. I declare Jesus is the Lord of my life. In Jesus's name, amen."

The fire of God's liberty is real. It isn't like the freedom the world speaks of. Adoption is the heart of who God is. Being adopted myself, my heart is comforted knowing God's heart about adoption and that

> when the fullness of time had come, God sent forth his Son, born of woman, born under the law, to redeem those who were under the law, so that we might receive adoption as sons. And because we are sons, God has sent the Spirit of his Son into our hearts, crying, "Abba! Father!" So, you are no longer a slave, but a son, and if a son, then an heir through God. (Gal. 4:4–6 ESV)

We never have to live as if we were unwanted orphans. God's heart is for us to be found in him. Being adopted into God's family means that Christ is now in us. With Christ in us, we can live in assurance that we can say no to sin and yes to righteous living and that we'll bear the fruit of the Holy Spirit, who is fully God and who has chosen to make his home in our hearts.

Ponder the magnitude of these words: the Holy Spirit lives in us. We can get comfortable abiding in a new dwelling and find encouragement in a new reality that heaven's deposit inside us will always be greater than hell's obstruction in front of us. "Ye are of God, little children, and have overcome them: because greater is he that is in you, than he that is in the world" (1 John 4:4 KJV).

Sometimes, we choose wrong because we simply don't fully understand our options in the situation and we just want to decide. When faced with a tough choice, we can go to Christ to seek wisdom to make sound choices. There is no design flaw when we walk in the Spirit of God. We can stop letting people put limitations and labels on us. We are who God says we are, and we can do what he says we can do. We can grow, become established, and advance his kingdom on earth for his glory.

Our salvation through Jesus is vital, critical; it's the clear and nonnegotiable precursor to accessing our inheritance. There are not many ways to God, and we can't choose to work only what works best for us. This is a popular and perpetuated lie of the enemy he uses to deceive the world. The enemy wants to steal heaven's citizens, so we must be serious about securing our salvation through Christ. Once we have our salvation in order, we can secure our identity. Reclaiming our spiritual authority is all about rising into our true identities and co-laboring with Christ for what's ours.

Rising looks like acceptance. It is accepting and declaring, "I am more than a conqueror!" (meditate on Rom. 8:37 NIV), "I am chosen, royal!" (meditate on 1 Peter 2:9 NIV), "I am loved by God!" (meditate on Jer. 31:3 NIV), "God promises to provide for me!" (meditate on Matt. 6:33 NIV), "I have access to angelic help!" (meditate on Ps. 91:11 NIV). This is holiness. This is being in right standing with God and is like gasoline is to fire.

The level of fulfillment every person seeks begins with seeking the King and his kingdom: "But seek ye first the kingdom of God, and his righteousness; and all these things shall be added unto you" (Matt. 6:33 KJV). You can never discover who you are and fulfill your purpose until you discover who God is. Peter's revelation of who Jesus was opened his eyes to his own purpose.

> When Jesus came to the region of Caesarea Philippi, he asked his disciples, "Who do people say the Son of Man is?" They replied, "Some say John the Baptist; others say Elijah; and still others, Jeremiah or one of the prophets." "But what about you?" he asked. "Who do you say

I am?" Simon Peter answered, "You are the Messiah, the Son of the living God." Jesus replied, "Blessed are you, Simon son of Jonah, for this was not revealed to you by flesh and blood, but by my Father in heaven. And I tell you that you are Peter, and on this rock I will build my church, and the gates of Hades will not overcome it. I will give you the keys of the kingdom of heaven; whatever you bind on earth will be bound in heaven, and whatever you loose on earth will be loosed in heaven." Then he ordered his disciples not to tell anyone that he was the Messiah. (Matt. 16:13–20 NIV)

We are not physically walking alongside Jesus as Peter did; only the Bible, God's Word, and his activation of it by the Holy Spirit will satisfy our soul. We don't have the power to live in his attributes or love without his sanctifying life in us. His life in us delivers us from the law, and we shift into faith so we can live supernaturally. The gospel of Jesus brings forgiveness and life, and we can connect to the gospel in such a way that we know Jesus loves us and his purpose for us. God loved us on our worst day, and he wants the world, which has rejected him, to be reconciled to himself. Therefore, he wants us to accept him in our hearts and keep him in our remembrance.

As children of God, we offer ourselves as living sacrifices when we hear his voice rather than hardening our hearts so Jesus can live in and through us and rejoice in being forgiven and new. It's as simple as saying, "I have learned to live with a 'Yes Lord.'" There are times of wrestling, but I remain yielded to him so I can become his daughter formed in the image of Christ and be the warrior I've been called to be.

We must daily decide to focus on and be a strong voice for God. We can become so yielded that we do as we're commanded even when it affects our emotions. We accept Christ's life in us by receiving him in our hearts and appropriating this life by faith. This consistent activation in our lives—believing Jesus is Lord and not just Savior—always follows the same sequences as salvation: "If you declare with your mouth, 'Jesus is LORD,' and believe in your heart that God raised him from the dead, you will be saved" (Rom. 10:9 NIV). We are to hear the word of truth, believe in our hearts, confess with our mouths, and do what the Word says.

Think of the depths of human nature, of human life. Think of the depths of the wells in you. Have you been impoverishing the ministry of Jesus so he cannot do anything? We impoverish his ministry the moment we forget he is the Almighty. We can make a better effort to look to him.

Many souls have gotten out of intimate contact with God by leaning on their own religious understanding. They often make commonsense decisions and ask God to bless them, but they are not told to walk in the light of conscience or out of a sense of duty but to walk in the light as God is in the light.

We cannot deal all by ourselves with the things that disturb our souls. We forget that Jesus does not work in commonsense ways but in supernatural ways. Is it possible to be so identified with him that there is nothing of our old lives left? Would we rather worry than believe God can and will do the impossible? The Word of the Lord pierces even to the dividing asunder of the soul and spirit until there is no deception left. If there is no hurt, if there are no impossible things, we miss out on great points of revelation. As we allow our minds to be controlled by his Spirit, we will have life and peace.

Through Jesus's blood, we have been reconciled to God and filled with life and peace the world cannot give. We are no longer ruled by darkness or the enemy's attacks; through Jesus, we are equipped to do what pleases God and cooperate with his will. If we trust in the sacrifice of Jesus and confess our sins, he will be faithful and just; he will forgive our sins and purify us of all unrighteousness. We don't have to fear any accusations of the enemy when we hold fast to Jesus. God can do exceedingly and abundantly above all that we can ask him for or imagine. He is faithful to watch over his Word and perform it in our lives.

Jesus chose twelve disciples to share a deeper level of intimacy with him, and out of the twelve, he took three—Peter, James, and John—into situations that none of the others had shared. "Six days later Jesus took with Him Peter and James and John the brother of James, and led them up on a high mountain by themselves" (Matt. 17:1 AMP). Of the three, only John felt comfortable enough to rest his head on Jesus's chest as he listened to the Lord talk at the Passover Feast: "One of His disciples, whom Jesus loved (esteemed), was leaning against Jesus' chest" (John 13:23 AMP).

When Jesus was dying on the cross, he told John to take care of his mother. He knew John loved him enough to do whatever he asked of him. Although Jesus loved all, there were few who were willing to make the same level of commitment as those who entered a more intimate relationship with him.

Not everyone is willing to obey God and pay the price required to be close to him, but God does not ask for all our time; however, he does ask to be kept first place at all times. We will not experience instant gratification when we seek God. We must sow before we reap; we must invest before we get a return. We must give up time before we can experience intimacy with God. An example of this is Mary: "Mary seated herself at the Lord's feet and was listening to his teaching" (Luke 10:49 AMP). Unlike Martha, her sister who was too busy to take time to enjoy Jesus when he came to her home, Mary seized the opportunity to sit at Jesus's feet and learn from him. Mary knew that work would always be there but Jesus would not. Like Martha, we can make the mistake of trying to work God into our schedules rather than putting him first and working the rest of our schedule around our time with him.

Not spending time with God is a mistake we often make in our spiritual lives. God tells us, "Those who hope in the LORD will renew their strength. They will soar on wings like eagles; they will run and not grow weary, they will walk and not be faint" (Isa. 40:31 NIV). When we spend time studying God's Word, praying, and growing in intimacy with him, he will change us and make us strong enough to endure whatever challenges come our way. We really can't move forward well in life if we don't choose the Lord as our portion as Mary did.

When Billy Graham, a great father of the faith, was asked in an interview if he would have done anything differently in his life, he said,

> I would study more. I would pray more, travel less, take less speaking engagements ... I took too many of them in too many places around the world. If I had to do it over again, I'd spend more time in meditation and prayer and just telling the Lord how much I love him.

Graham had an inspiring heart position of humility and a walk of integrity before God.

Our next level depends on our humility, the attitude of our hearts and minds that God requires of us. We are never to consider ourselves as better than or above other people. According to Proverbs, a proud person overestimates himself and underestimates others; he has "haughty eyes, a lying tongue, hands that shed innocent blood" (Prov. 6:17 NIV). It's better to think the best of others and be wrong rather than think the worst of others and be wrong. If we think more highly of ourselves than we ought and exaggerate our importance, we will see others as beneath us. That can cause us to have a disrespectful attitude and harsh behavior toward others even our family and friends.

Strive to give God what he truly requires, which is to do what is just, love mercy and kindness, and to walk humbly with him. Pride—arrogant self-sufficiency—is the number one sin because it keeps you from recognizing your need for a Savior. You live with a sense of superiority, and no one lives up to how great you are; that disconnects you from people and compromises God's mission. Unlike humility, pride blinds you to your faults. It lashes out and lives superficially. It's completely and utterly self-centered. Humility is making the noble choice to not be that way and to use your influence to serve and bless.

At all costs, you must be rightly related to God. This is the flow you want, but it takes a decision and fixed commitment to position yourself in God's system and intensely focus on his point of view. It is becoming one with Jesus so the nature that controlled him will control you.

This also means restricting our earthly concerns and expanding our godly concerns. With humility, we can accept divine resets and daily self-checks so the Holy Spirit gets the right of way in our lives and we can live lives that please our Creator. As Paul said, "For you know that we dealt with each of you as a father deals with his own children, encouraging, comforting and urging you to live lives worthy of God, who calls you into his kingdom and glory" (1 Thess. 2:12 NIV).

Here is a sample divine reset that could replace the common vision boarding that we've likely heard about. The purpose of the reset is to check in monthly on how well you're depending on Christ.

DIVINE RESET

1. Realize that God has given you power. "I have given you authority to trample on snakes and scorpions and to overcome all the power of the enemy; nothing will harm you" (Luke 10:19 NIV).

2. Refocus your priorities. It takes great faith to stay in a state of knowing God has you covered and to sit and soak in his presence rather than trying to be the great problem solver. "So do not worry, saying, 'What shall we eat?' or 'What shall we drink?' or 'What shall we wear?' For the pagans run after all these things, and your heavenly Father knows that you need them" (Matt. 6:31–32 NIV).

3. Remember Christ has set you free. "It is for freedom that Christ has set us free. Stand firm, then, and do not let yourselves be burdened again by a yoke of slavery" (Gal. 5:1 NIV).

Like the monthly divine reset, you can check yourself daily during your quiet time to remain confident that he who began a good work in you will carry it to completion. Self-checks are a surefire way to assess whether you are depending on yourself and leaning on your own understanding to carry out the work in and around you or whether you are depending on God.

SELF-CHECKS

1. Am I still operating in my own strength?
2. Have I set myself apart, or do I resemble the world?
3. Do I carry a positive testimony? If I am a saint, am I acting like one? Live as a positive testimony to the name/family you represent.
4. How is my fellowship with my Father?

The soul is liable to distractions and agitations, but the closer and more intimate your relationship with God becomes, the more clearly you'll hear him speak. God's peace will preserve your mind when you start believing he is directing your steps. Believe he is controlling your life and you reduce your agenda down to one thing—reflecting him. The peace of God will calm every agitated part of your soul. If you don't have peace, don't move.

No matter how we may feel or what our attitude may be toward God, we are bound as creatures dependent on his love and favor. We constantly have to allow him to come back center in our hearts. In these times of uncertainty and change, when distraction, fear, and shame become constant temptations, God is looking for those who stand steady, who are anchored in

Christ, and who operate in the power of the Holy Spirit and face the future confident in the love of the Father.

The Bible says, "The godly walk with integrity; blessed are their children who follow them" (Prov. 20:7 NLT). Also, "Those who belong to Christ Jesus have nailed the passions and desires of their sinful nature to his cross and crucified them there" (Gal. 5:24 NLT). To test our integrity, we need to see how much we are trusting God and what we keep in our hearts daily.

Hypocrisy is the gap between what we show and who we are. I don't want a gap. When I became intentional about being real about him, that affected my walk with him. I decided I would courageously look at anything I was carrying or demonstrating that could be hindering my witness. I was led to create two columns on some paper and make it part of my daily time with God. I would write out all my cares before I went into prayer so there would be nothing blocking our time, and I would trust that by the end of my seeking him, I would be led to scripture that would counter all my cares. I would start with this prayer as a guide: "Search me, O God, and know my heart; test me and know my anxious thoughts. Point out anything in me that offends you, and lead me along the path of everlasting life" (Ps. 139:23–24 NLT).

My Cares to Cast	God's Promises to Stand On
Work—Changing demands, unclear expectations, instability	"Commit your work to the LORD and your plans will be established" (Prov. 16:3 ESV).

Relationships—Battling expectations and distrust	"Blessed is the man who trusts in the LORD, whose trust is the LORD. He is like a tree planted by water, that sends out its roots by the stream, and does not fear when heat comes, for its leaves remain green, and is not anxious in the year of drought, for it does not cease to bear fruit" (Jer. 17:7–8 ESV).
Finances—Made several big investments and still waiting on a return	"And my God will supply every need of yours according to his riches in glory in Christ Jesus" (Phil. 4:19 ESV).
Self—Negative self-talk, yo-yo eating, and resisting workouts	"I have been crucified with Christ. It is no longer I who live, but Christ who lives in me" (Gal. 2:20 NIV).

By conducting this exercise daily, I quickly saw how much faith I was full of and where my work with the Lord needed to be focused. God is the wisest and the most merciful person in the universe; I think we'd all be wise to trust his attribute of self-control and meditate on this: "Better a patient person than a warrior, one with self-control than one who takes a city" (Prov. 16:32 NIV).

Self-control requires humility. We can learn to meditate on the Word until we are inundated with the thoughts of God. We can also dare to believe him for big things. I've grown to enjoy this practice, and I've noticed the Holy Spirit is always gentle yet firm in his conviction and steady in his commitment to my growth. He meets my willingness to be transformed and never fails to be a reliable companion in my ongoing transformation.

God wants us to keep returning to him, our home base, our place of safety and refuge where we can boldly and confidently deal with all we carry beneath the surface. He never cares how far we've run; he just wants us to keep coming back to him so he can give us what we need.

Leadership is not about me, my success, or my name; it's about God's glory. This chart can help you discover the characteristics you're demonstrating and the truths an equipped leader needs to be successful, fight through negativity, and stay committed when faced with challenges.

Is anything too hard for the Lord? We can determine not to allow the enemy to magnify the difficulties in our lives and make them appear unconquerable. We must practice shaking off the enemy's lies. We can make up our minds that no anxious thought will sway our focus. We should remember we are blessed, chosen, and secure under Jesus's blood. We can cast our cares knowing that nothing is too insignificant for the Lord and that he will raise us up in peace and security. The Father says about you only what the blood of Jesus reminds him about you. Remember, "Blessed are those who trust in the Lord and have made the Lord their hope and confidence" (Jer. 17:7 NLT).

As we cultivate God consciousness, we develop his confidence in us and are clear and uncompromising about who we are and where we're headed. God is our gap filler. He can fill the emptiness wherever we see it because in him there is no darkness. Whatever we do, we should never miss where God is. Access to the Word is a privilege, and it's vital for our lives. Smart people submit to the leadership of the Holy Spirit.

We can boldly consult with God, our master coach, every day. Unlike a life coach, God commands that he be number one and that we guard against put anything ahead of him that will keep us from letting Jesus coach us. Winning in the Christian life takes coaching, endurance, and focus.

There are practical things you can do to strengthen and position yourself for victory: "If anyone is in Christ, the new creation has come: The old has gone, the new is here! All this is from God, who reconciled us to himself through Christ and gave us the ministry of reconciliation" (2 Cor. 5:17–18 NIV).

To reconcile means to change, to make things right. You signed up to receive Christ, then you gave God all that you are, and now you invite God to form you and coach you through the ongoing process of sanctification. You are not conformed to the world and its ways but are being constantly transformed by renewing your mind. You are to be formed into Christlikeness and his kingdom qualities; he is reshaping you. You are also transformed to discern God's perfect will is. He is forming the life he has for you, and you are developing the mind of Christ; in developing it, you are in Christ, the perfect will and plan of God. He didn't put you together accidently; being transformed is a process.

You know how to physically get in shape, but the most important conditioning you can do is with your soul. This is how the Holy Spirit coaches you as you are in Christ. How many times has he tried to speak to you and give you instruction but you didn't hear or listen? As you grow and mature, you follow through in the formation of your mind effectively and efficiently as you get out of the way.

Not all can grow in him because not all are coachable; they want to run their own lives. When you receive Christ, you choose to be coachable. Some can't grow and mature in him and experience all the freedom and joy he has for them. They don't believe they can change or even need to. They are selective listeners and selectively let him run their lives; they are reluctant to let him have full access. They need to get to the place where they put it all on the altar and surrender their lives to him. Those who become completely coachable will be able to withstand all the pressures and bullying they come up against.

Being willing to give God your yes requires three things.

UNDERSTANDING

You need understanding not about what he is calling you to but about who he is and how he operates. Some things will not make sense until you get there, so understand that you do not have to have it all figured out before you get there; you just need to know who is speaking to you, and then you move.

God already has a vision for your life, and he is reliable and trustworthy. You won't get there by him showing you but by listening to him. Your destiny is tied to your yes. Understanding says you cannot become what God wants you to become without your yes with no strings attached. He will not give much beyond instructions; there may be a little affirmation, but once he gives instruction, that's it; he doesn't have a plan B for you. Only he can speak it to you. Sometimes, you may be tempted to trade destiny for company, for the familiar, for the way things were. But trust in God. You want heaven's applause; don't live for the applause of anyone else.

BELIEF

Belief is a big deal. You may be pursuing God and trying to figure out what is right and wrong, but "Abram believed the

Lord, and he credited it to him as righteousness" (Gen. 15:6 NIV). It was nothing that Abram did; it was the fact that he believed. You won't give God your yes if you don't trust him. You have enough confirmation already, so will you step out or not? Will you be righteous in your belief? Destiny unfolds in steps.

SENSITIVITY

Sensitivity is cultivated and developed through your relationship with God, and it gradually teaches you to discern and understand his voice. You gradually connect what you're feeling to what God is saying or acknowledge what you're feeling is God. God has made you sensitive enough to learn and understand how to understand his voice. You learn how to connect what you are intuiting in your gut to the voice of God so you can give a timely yes.

You must know how to hear God. There is no course on this, but you are wired to hear the voice of your Creator. A perfect example of this is Samuel, who was being called by the Lord but did not yet know his voice, so his friend Eli taught him how to respond the next time he heard the Lord. Eli said to Samuel, "Go lie down, and it shall be if He calls you, that you shall say, 'Speak, LORD, for Your servant is listening'" (1 Sam. 3:10 NASB).

Once you dispel distractions and be still, you will be able to hear the word the Lord has for you. When you are still, you can experience God with expectancy rather than anxiety. You will be positioned to hear his voice; this is everything because you cannot say yes to what you do not receive.

The rest is trial and error. Learn from the times you didn't listen when you knew you should have. As you walk with

God long enough and you give him these yeses, you'll become more sensitive. The more you say yes, the more God will feed you his daily manna. Give him your heart, obedience, and yes responses all along the way. His instruction will always elevate you.

Success for the purposes of this book is being abandoned to Christ and co-laboring with him. With this as the new definition of success, we will find that joy is being continually refreshed in him. God gives us what we need to behave correctly and has invested his power in our spiritual growth. Sometimes, it takes a painful experience to make us change our ways, but it doesn't always require that. The miracle of redemption is that God turns us unholy ones into the standard of himself by putting us into the disposition of Jesus Christ.

You will know you are living a set-apart life when you are not aloof but are living in another world. Just like Jesus, you will strive to never allow anything to interfere with your concentration of spiritual energy. You will be interested in what God is interested in, and there will be no dull moments when the king is with you.

It's time to walk out of the wilderness of you. "The LORD our God spoke to us at Horeb, saying, 'You have stayed long enough on this mountain'" (Deut. 1:6 AMP). Moses pointed this word out to the Israelites—it was only an eleven-day journey to the border of their Promised Land, Canaan, yet it had taken them forty years to get there.

Moses was led to wake up the Israelites and help them realize they were going nowhere. They had many wrong mind-sets and many mental strongholds they'd built up over the years that were keeping them from all God had for them. They didn't realize that the enemy had been lying to them, that they had believed him and had been deceived. The Israelites stayed in the wilderness because they had a wilderness mentality—wrong thinking kept them in bondage.

Can you relate? You have to exercise self-control to make quality decisions to renew your mind and learn to choose your thoughts carefully. Make up your mind to not give up until victory is complete and you have taken possession of your rightful inheritance. Do not stay too long in any one place; keep moving toward everything God has for you.

Wholeness says, "I'm glad you know Jesus, but in recognizing wholeness, you must also recognize and assess the damage done by your years of brokenness and the seasons of injustice you endured living in the enemy's reality separated from Jesus." The last thing the enemy of your soul wants is for you to be whole. He'd much rather continue to subtly operate under the radar because if you can't see him, he can exploit you.

Fear—the opposite of God and love—distorts who we are. When we operate in our authority, we will still experience fear, but we will refuse to take the enemy's bait and worry and go forward. What type of servants would we be if we sacrificed our identities and inheritances as children of God for our comfort? In uncomfortable and disruptive times, we must allow Jesus to show us what is in us. We should ask, "If I make this choice, will people see me walking in the power of the gospel?" God is always trying to bless us, but we won't see that unless we take control of the narrative we're telling ourselves.

Don't miss your call, your increase, or your elevation. Don't let the enemy talk you out of your blessing. Instead of looking for someone to show up and be strong, recognize that you are who you've been looking for. Realize that you are on this planet for a purpose and your reality identity is spiritual, so don't get caught up in anything else. Get down to the real you. Anything you're after will come from the inside. You don't have to doubt that God put something in you, but it will take certain things to get that level of you to rise.

Tell yourself the truth; you need that as a way for who you are. You are defined by the anointing of God on your life, and you must always have this as a reason for the hope in front of you so you'll be inspired to fight and not just let things happen to you.

It's not easy, but if you make strong choices, you'll start a movement of strong people. Jesus is strong for us. Christ died for the ungodly: "Very rarely will anyone die for a righteous person, though for a good person someone might possibly dare to die. But God demonstrates his own love for us in this: While we were still sinners, Christ died for us" (Rom. 5:7–8 NIV).

God can't wait to see you know and embrace all he's called you to be. It's time to thrive, not just survive. Any sin that could block your spiritual inner sensitivities to God could hinder your progress and destiny. Trust that God has a good plan for you far greater than you've imagined. Humble yourself under God's mighty hand so he can lift you up in due time (1 Peter 5:6).

PROMPT FOR REFLECTION

Where are you trying to play God's role in your life?

PRAYER

By God's grace, may I eliminate hurry and worry in my life. May I instead slow my pace and turn my face to the one who loves, saves, redeems, and restores everything about me. Instead of grabbing for myself, may I wait to see how God provides and cares for me. May I enter a new season in which

I know God's rest, pace, and provision like I've never known. He's for me and with me in ways I can't even imagine! "What no eye has seen, what no ear has heard, and what no human mind has conceived ... the things God has prepared for those who love him" (1 Cor. 2:9 NIV).

Chapter 2

The Call

> Therefore, since we are surrounded by such a great cloud of witnesses, let us throw off everything that hinders and the sin that so easily entangles. And let us run with perseverance the race marked out for us, fixing our eyes on Jesus, the pioneer and perfecter of faith. For the joy set before him he endured the cross, scorning its shame, and sat down at the right hand of the throne of God.
> —Hebrews 12:1-2 (NIV)

Now that Jesus has found a home in your heart and you've placed all your trust in the one who died and rose again, you're ready for the responsibility of the call. When the vision of where you're headed is clear enough, it will draw you forward through every challenge and over every obstacle, but "when people do not accept divine guidance, they run wild. But whoever obeys the law is joyful" (Prov. 29:18 NLT). When you consider the call, start with vision. The Old Testament prophet Habakkuk received divine revelation regarding vision when he was commanded to write the vision and make it plain on tablets, that he may run who reads it. For the vision is yet for an appointed time; but at the end it will speak, and it will not lie. Though it tarries, wait for it; because it will surely come, it will not tarry. (Hab. 2:2 NKJV)

If God's prophet needed revelation, how much more do we need it in our times? We need vision to operate and a clear understanding of the identity God has spoken over our lives to yield and wield the power we've been given with excellence and precision. We must be trained and enabled to fearlessly wield the sword of the Lord. The Holy Spirit will work with those who work with him and leave to themselves those who will not.

If we have hearing ears and seeing eyes to receive the Holy Spirit's revelation, we can be properly prepared to participate supernaturally in our lives. If we have these qualities, we also have the challenge of walking in obedience to this new truth as it is given. It is deeper than just a relationship with Christ; it is walking step by step with him guided by the light of his prophetic words. The apostle Paul's desire was that we receive the full enlightenment of our inheritance to know the hope of our calling: "I pray that the eyes of your heart may be enlightened in order that you may know the hope to which he has called you, the riches of his glorious inheritance in his holy people" (Eph. 1:18 NIV).

Your vision could simply be letting your life demonstrate the power of working with God. Cooperation with God is simply splitting your life's work with him and getting it done. Your part is consecration and acts of obedience, and God's part is sanctification. He will purify you from the inside out to be like Christ and give you the grace through his Holy Spirit to walk out your salvation.

I hope you're firmly grounded in your God-ordained identity. With that tight and right, you will have a pure and humble heart ready to trust in God as he leads you in every endeavor. As you walk boldly and courageously in God's identity for your life, you will receive his strength and wisdom for strategically pressing on.

God is looking for those who will exemplify confidence in Christ, boldness in the battle, and valor to win the victory for the kingdom of God. Jesus is committed to co-laboring with his church. The Holy Spirit wants to help strengthen you in your calling, stir you, and guide you in understanding your place in God's world. His teaching is always anti self-realization and pro Christ-realization.

Once you've found your identity and authority in Christ, you will build your relationship with Jesus through trusting and resting in him and co-laboring with him; you will embrace the spiritual disciplines that bring freedom and glory in every area of your life. This is the wonderful new; you're so committed to staying in alignment and co-laboring with Christ that without realizing it, you break out of the old patterns and beliefs you once trusted and perceive the wonderful: "For I am about to do something new. See, I have already begun! Do you not see it? I will make a pathway through the wilderness. I will create rivers in the dry wasteland" (Isa. 43:19 NLT). You will know if the Spirit has drawn you out of the world systems, infused you with truth, and made you a radical warrior in his kingdom movement on earth if you identity with these qualities.

- a burning desire to be all God has called you to be
- a yearning to fulfill your highest potential in Christ

- an eagerness to leave your imprint and make a difference
- a willingness to explore each life area and determine how you can be most effective in each as you pursue God's call on your life
- a desire to change patterns of repression and unrighteousness and shift out of bondage into freedom and life
- a hunger to hear God's voice and impact the world
- a readiness for deliverance from the strongholds of excuses and personally inflicted constraints that have kept you from fulfilling God's highest purpose for your life
- a willingness to embrace God's vision for your life
- a commitment to use the authority given you to conquer and overcome situations that would otherwise seem unconquerable

Everything God has done on earth since the creation of humankind requires our participating with him to bring it to pass. God is waiting on us. To bring change, we must be willing to endure change, implement change, and be full of God's vision for our future.

In every area of your life, you want to have an impact. You want to know that your living isn't in vain. This comes down to vision—monitoring it and keeping it in plain sight. You want to be busy living your life but not so busy that you're wondering where all the time has gone.

When we focus our energy and efforts, we can enable the last half of our lives to be the best half of our lives. God's vision for us is that we be salt and light in the world.

> You are the salt of the earth. But if the salt loses its saltiness, how can it be made salty again? It is no longer good for anything, except to be

> thrown out and trampled underfoot. You are the light of the world. A town built on a hill cannot be hidden. Neither do people light a lamp and put it under a bowl. Instead they put it on its stand, and it gives light to everyone in the house. In the same way, let your light shine before others, that they may see your good deeds and glorify your Father in heaven. (Matt. 5:13–16 NIV)

We can either starve or nourish the life in us. When we did not know God, we were slaves to those who by nature were not gods.

> But now that you know God—or rather are known by God—how is it that you are turning back to those weak and miserable forces? Do you wish to be enslaved by them all over again? You are observing special days and months and seasons and years! I fear for you, that somehow I have wasted my efforts on you. (Gal. 4:9–11 NIV)

But since we are God's we,

> are no longer a slave, but God's child; and since you are his child, God has made you also an heir. (Gal. 4:7 NIV)

God guarantees that an inheritance waits for us because we are his children. Collaborating with God changes the dynamics; we must keep our appointments with our master coach as if our lives depended upon it because they do.

Our call is to a higher ground in the glory of the Lord where we think on Jesus and make him the center of it all. Our power is in our continual look at God.

Live through the Spirit's power and live confidently in the hope that things will be put right through faith. Belief in God energized by love makes a difference. Nothing is as important as keeping right spiritually and intense devotion to be God's new creation. God will not deny any good thing to those who live with integrity.

Our calls don't really relate to a ministry but to doing certain things in certain areas God has called us to. As ambassadors for Christ, salt and light, we're all in the same full-time ministry.

Whatever it is you're specifically called to do be it in the professional or entertainment world for example, a lifestyle in the Spirit has been set aside for you, and there are gifts and anointings God wants to bestow on you so you can do the best possible job in partnership with Jesus. You will need to endure a training process for the place God is taking you. All God wants is your yes to forsake your former manner of living for the new life that God can live through you. He wants you to rely on your master toolkit, the Bible, and be a doer of the Word. You don't have to be qualified or know what to do; you simply have to accept that God knows whom he's calling and you respond to him. God is the fulfillment of my life—can you claim that too?

The Holy Spirit pushes us to the margins of our individuality, and we either deny him access or surrender to his work. We never have to limp through life when Jesus is at its center. God wants to bring us into union with himself, but unless we are willing to give up our right to ourselves, he cannot.

Will you let your personal life and personality be brought into fellowship with God? This means your individuality; your independence and self-assertiveness have to be put in the grace of God so that grace can live in you. Ask yourself, *What's unsettling in me? Where am I being found faithful? Where am I expecting God to show up?* Only God can understand you fully. In relationship with him, you truly begin to understand that love is the outpouring of his personality in fellowship with your personality.

To walk in the Spirit means to order our lives around the Holy Spirit. We follow his lead and keep in step with what he is doing in our lives. We find real excitement in life in Jesus.

As I walked with God, I noticed rather than answering all my questions, he started asking me questions. This one got me: *What is your biggest dream?* My answer surprised me. I wanted to see God's hand move in a great convergence in my life. I wanted to see the manifestation of the promises I'd been praying over the years and redemption of the different experiences I was graced to endure. I wanted to witness him move in such an intimate and personal way that it increased my faith. I wanted to know that all my stepping out wasn't just wishful thinking. And right at the end of my reflection on and answering my own questions as led by the Holy Spirit, God got me. He revealed I still had trust issues. I still needed to be reminded of God's love for me and become more firmly rooted and grounded in that. I was still allowing myself to believe I was an afterthought to God, not an answer to something significant.

Loyalty to Jesus is the one thing we cringe at. We will be loyal to work, to service, to anything, but do not ask us to be loyal to Jesus. But regardless of us, God is still a miracle worker and a promise keeper. He wasn't surprised by my secret, but he also didn't want me to live a lie any longer. He wanted me to truly enjoy life as it unfolded.

Redemption creates the life of God in us, so it creates the things belonging to that life. He heals our faithlessness and loves us freely. It's not that we are to do work for God but that we are to be so loyal to him that he can do his work through us. Jesus came to send a sword through every peace that was not based on a personal relationship with himself.

If you will continually humble yourself and yield to him, God will be your everlasting light and the God of your glory. Every choice you make on some level determines the standards you set for yourself and your life. Decide definitively the standards for what you're willing to accept in life. Are they God's standards? If not, raise your standards, set your boundaries, and allow yourself to entertain only what is good, empowering, and beautiful in your life. From there, you can start to make more-powerful and informed choices that are aligned with the type of person you want to be and the type of life you want to live. Otherwise, you will shape-shift and move further away from what you deserve.

Never nourish an experience that doesn't have God as its source and faith in God as a result. Is Jesus the Lord of your experiences, or do you try to hand it over to him? Where the enemy consistently attacks your heart shows you where you struggle to keep God first. Satan will constantly dangle people, things, and desires in front of you—anything to distract you so he can erect a false god in front of you that you didn't realize you had. He will try to lure you with a false god such as a career, a spouse or love interest, a dream or goal, a hobby or lifestyle—anything to prevent you from rightly relating with God and prevent God from working in you. It's a subtle way of starting to love other things more than God—even a feeling.

Don't let Satan try to sneak anything else front and center. Your worries make you doubt God's love and provision. Satan wants you stressing rather than resting in God's ability to care for you. Nothing and no one should crowd out God's peace in your life or push you to the point that you begin to believe God for your circumstances.

The enemy wants you to look just like the world, so he starts with your daily thinking. He wants you professing that you know and follow God, but your thinking looks nothing like him. He wants subtle messages, music, lyrics, statements, and words of advice from friends (even friends who are believers) to shift your focus.

When you commit to living a consecrated life, you can expect your enemy to turn up the heat, so guard your thinking by soaking it in scripture. Don't be naive or surprised if the enemy goes after your speech so you tear others apart. The enemy wants you blowing it big time with your mouth rather than being a holy mouthpiece for God. It may seem harmless, but a few critical words here, a few complaints there, some profanity mixed in with a little gossip on the side and you have given him permission to make you someone who tears others apart and sounds the same as and sometimes worse than unbelievers. Close that door.

> Do not let any unwholesome talk come out of your mouths, but only what is helpful for building others up according to their needs, that it may benefit those who listen. (Eph. 4:29 NIV)

> Give thanks in all circumstances; for this is God's will for you in Christ Jesus. (1 Thess. 5:18 NIV)

Don't be surprised if the enemy goes after your body so it no longer glorifies God. Don't let the enemy harm, mutilate, starve, or destroy what God has called holy. Don't let him determine how you dress, see yourself, or treat yourself.

> Therefore, I urge you, brothers and sisters, in view of God's mercy, to offer your bodies as a living sacrifice, holy and pleasing to God—this is your true and proper worship. (Rom. 12:1 NIV)

> Do you not know that your bodies are temples of the Holy Spirit, who is in you, whom you have received from God? You are not your own; you were bought at a price. Therefore honor God with your bodies. (1 Cor. 6:19–20 NIV)

Don't be surprised if the enemy goes after your beliefs to shake your trust in God and make you rely only on your own limited understanding. To believe, you have to be ready to disassociate from your old ways of looking at things and lean yourself entirely on God.

> If any of you lack wisdom, let him ask of God, that giveth to all [men] liberally, and upbraideth not; and it shall be given him. (James 1:5–6 KJV)

> And he believed in the LORD; and he counted it to him for righteousness. (Gen. 15:6 KJV)

Every now and again, God lets us see what we would be like if it were not for him and his work in our lives. The most secure thing is to live a sanctified life because it has the almighty God behind it. If we are born again, it is the easiest thing to live in right relationship with God and the most difficult thing to go wrong; we just have to heed God's warnings and keep in the light. When we are born again, we yield ourselves so completely to God that Jesus is formed in us—his nature will immediately begin to work through us.

To walk in the light means that everything in darkness drives us closer to the light. "But if we walk in the light, as he is in the light, we have fellowship with one another, and the blood of Jesus, his Son, purifies us from all sin" (1 John 1:7 NIV).

God's way is so much better than we can imagine. We can be so accustomed to evaluating success by this or that or how much or how many, but sometimes, success can simply be the fact that we are in a place stabilizing what would have become contaminated or dysfunctional had he not been there as a barrier. Our presence is our impact. We are so much more than what we do; what a wonderful truth that is.

Leading and stewarding your call are determined by functionality, and how you function in your call must be measured. If you don't have any reference of measurement active in your life, how do you know whether you're having an impact and are in alignment with God's will and plan for you? When you have a strong sense of where you are and how you measure up, you will guard against depression, stress, worry, anxiety, and confusion.

Many people who do not measure their impact acutely measure their energy. We'll know this when we hear, "I'm tired," "This job is driving me crazy," and "I'm not appreciated for all the work I've been putting in." We are taught to measure our impact by how it affects our energy. After a while, if we are looking only at what we are giving and not considering what has come back, the fruits of our efforts, we start losing our saltiness.

When we set our eyes only on what we see and where we are comparatively in the different areas of our lives, we miss out on the actual picture that can be found only when we fix our eyes on Jesus, who has an impact, so it makes sense to study and pattern ourselves after him. Unfortunately, our focus tends to wander and we tend to grab more than we can maintain. That requires our getting over our agendas, quitting the chase after more, and saying no to things we could do but God hasn't led us to do.

The most powerful people are those who have learned to say no: "But let your 'Yes' be 'Yes,' and your 'No,' 'No.' For whatever is more than these is from the evil one" (Matt. 5:37 NKJV). Sometimes, we feel overwhelmed by things we brought on ourselves by having said yes to more than we can handle. We teach people how to relate to us, so if we don't first deal with ourselves and measure our lives, we will inevitably invite imbalance. We should focus more on impact rather than what things cost us. If we don't learn to measure impact, it will affect how we do everything.

If we don't learn to think differently about the choices we make, we won't know when we're expending energy in areas where we are not impactful. Wouldn't it be better to know where we are not just gifted but impactful so we don't try to function in ways we are not gifted for? Does God really call us to do things we are not good at?

When we are impactful, supernatural things happen. It's important to grasp this because while we are putting our energy into areas where we may be weak, we do so at the expense of other areas where we are called and have the unique strengths and are equipped to fulfill tasks. Wouldn't it be helpful to connect with and be led by the one who knows all this before we step out into any opportunity?

Impact has a lot to do with perspective. We are at our best when we stop relying on how we feel and start relying on God, who fills us. Success doesn't always feel successful. Living a bold and impactful life will make us uncomfortable at times, but that's just growing pains and not the best barometer of overall success. "And we all, who with unveiled faces contemplate the Lord's glory, are being transformed into his image with ever-increasing glory, which comes from the Lord, who is the Spirit" (2 Cor. 3:18 NIV). If we believe our Christlikeness is our impact, the only way to increase in our Christlikeness is to increase our time and effort in pursuit of him and what matters to him.

Give yourself permission to be where you are, but let Jesus lead you to where he wants you to be. Jesus is the measure of our impact; no one else is; if no one else made us, no one else can rate us. The question is how much impact Jesus has on our lives. What in our lives competes with Jesus for control over us? Have we measured the metrics of impact with Jesus to really know where we are?

Even God has a means of measuring his impact; before he was done forming the earth, he had a little moment of celebration when he said, "It was good." God will never change; we can put all our security and confidence in the fact that he will never alter the way he sees or thinks and feels about us. Focusing on him and bringing him glory is a sure way to gauge what qualifies as impact. From the very beginning of a thing, we can assess the promise of the outcome we're after and prepare by working with the Holy Spirit to become the versions of ourselves that are ready to handle his promise.

We focus on the harvest before we plant the seed because God is the one who provides: "Now he who supplies seed to the sower and bread for food will also supply and increase your store of seed and will enlarge the harvest of your righteousness" (2

Cor. 9:10 NIV). In the same way, he will provide and increase our resources and produce a great harvest of generosity in us.

The apostle Paul was all about having real impact; many of his letters and visits to churches was all about encouragement from someone who lived an intentional life. He planned on the impact of his harvest before he sowed his seeds, and he adjusted the seed planting according to the level of impact he wanted to have. He didn't focus on how much energy that would cost him but on the lives he could stir up: "Therefore, I do not run like someone running aimlessly; I do not fight like a boxer beating the air" (1 Cor. 9:26 NLT). Running around aimlessly is being a jack of all trades but master of none. The enemy will always try to shame you in the area where God wants to use you, so the new you may have to put the old you in check.

We need to build our foundations and identities on the bedrock truth and God's love. The only way we realize we built our security on faulty foundations is when they are shaken. The shaking isn't for harm or destruction; the insecurity we feel is an invitation to achieve greater security in Christ. To make us more secure, God will allow insecurity to reveal false security and identity. The more we grow in our pursuit of Christlikeness, the more we will naturally live out our God-given roles. We grow when we fix our eyes on Jesus.

Sometimes, we affect what matters to us because we quit monitoring the impact we're making. Every so often, it's worth considering the level of impact we're having in different life areas because that will inform us how we can adjust. In a relationship for example, we can't assume that what we invested a couple of years ago would be enough to keep another person happy now. We need to monitor the relationship and determine how we can be flexible and adapt to its elevation and expansion or it will begin to deteriorate.

If our focus is on being salt, we will consider how to go out into our world and change everything we touch. We want whatever we're assigned to do to have an impact, and impact doesn't just happen; it's more than having good intentions. We must have a strategy and monitor if it works or not. If we don't monitor it, we will continue to put time, energy, and dollars into something that might not be working. We are limited resources and can focus only on so many things at a time, and God will not give us more life; he wants us to do more with the lives he's given us. If we want to have an impact and be effective, we must save our energy for what God requires.

Few are those who have taught us to steward our calls better than Paul, who told the Corinthians, "To the weak I became weak, to win the weak. I have become all things to all people so that by all possible means I might save some" (1 Cor. 9:22 NIV). Paul realized that he wouldn't be able to reach everyone but that he could reach some. He gauged his impact, and we too can become aware of what isn't working and change that.

Any time we want to change or we crave something to change in any area of our lives, we must have a new strategy. God knew this; that's why he gave us all the keys we would need to open new doors in his Word. He knew we couldn't go boldly into the new if we were carrying things that no longer suited where he was leading us. As we grow in Christ, we need to receive from every aspect of him, but what we think God requires of us and what he actually requires of us can be different. We might think God requires us to do a lot of church work or good deeds; we might think he requires extreme sacrifices or perfection from us. We might even think he requires us to read the Bible from Genesis to Revelation every year and spend hours each day in prayer and meditation.

Though these things can be good and have their place, we may do them and still miss what God considers important.

God's requirements are simple; we just tend to complicate them. His requirements have a lot to do with how we treat others. We are to do what is just, love mercy and kindness, and walk humbly with our God. God is just; he is always fair and works to make wrong things right. We should treat people justly and work to see justice done in their lives. Many people have been terribly treated and abused, but we can as God's representatives help them enjoy what Jesus died for them to have.

God also requires us to love mercy and kindness. We certainly need more kindness and mercy in the world. People do not need to be pressured to perform perfectly; they need to be loved and accepted. God's goodness, not his judgment, leads people to repentance. Our job is not to be faultfinders but to be dispensers of God's mercy and kindness. God is merciful and kind to us, and he expects us to give to other what we have received from him.

We want to have impact, but we must be willing to stretch and be fueled by the Holy Spirit. Only we can change our minds. The Holy Spirit in us will give us the power to do everything we need to do. When we have the Holy Spirit in us, we have a winning strategy.

The Holy Spirit offers insight into the Word and God's will, and that can change your life. Are you walking in a lack of understanding? The lens available through the Lord Jesus Christ can change everything: "What we have received is not the spirit of the world, but the Spirit who is from God, so that we may understand what God has freely given us" (1 Cor. 2:12 NIV).

The Holy Spirit gives us strength to obey with skill. We cannot honor God on our own. When we come to God, he gives us the strength we don't have. When we embrace the life Jesus has for us, we'll be amazed at what he can do through us. He gives us strength to overcome our sinful instincts so our lives will have simple, God-honoring patterns and will glorify him. "So I say, walk by the Spirit, and you will not gratify the desires of the flesh" (Gal. 5:16 NIV).

The Holy Spirit gives us gifts so we can really contribute to others' lives. Our prayers, our focus on God, and our obedience matter. He wants us to make a difference in the kingdom. We were created for contribution. He wants us at the center of his will for people in our world. "Now to each one the manifestation of the Spirit is given for the common good" (1 Cor. 12:7 NIV).

The Holy Spirit gives us leadership in daily life. He is our master motoring system because too many times, things are not black or white. Sometimes, what we think are indicators of God's leadership are not. As his sheep, we know our Shepherd's voice. Do we hear the Holy Spirit talking to us? He compels, inspires, and leads us: "My sheep listen to my voice; I know them, and they follow me" (John 10:27 NIV).

We walk in the greatest seasons of our lives when we obey the Holy Spirit, who can change anything. When we embrace Jesus, we can live lives of sustained momentum. We can be stronger, wiser, and more alert to the things of God because his favor is on our lives, but that requires us to repeatedly adjust to the Holy Spirit's promptings. We need to keep it our priority to be filled with and controlled by him.

As in any relationship, we can give up the power and momentum of walking with the Holy Spirit. The Bible says we can grieve the Spirit. We can sense the momentum change when we operate in negative energy, but we can confess our sins and immediately get back in control. We can also quench the Spirit when we say no to and ignore the Word of God.

We can be cold to the Word of God, but if we take the power we've been given and fix our eyes on him, we can advance. If the Spirit can raise Jesus from the dead, he can take us to and through our calls. The world cannot win against someone who is fueled by the Holy Spirit. We can hold our own with the best of them because we have power. Nothing remarkable can be achieved in our personal growth without being open to love and unleashing its joyful fire into the world.

There's power in leading by example. Invest your time and energy in whatever will contribute to your growth. Transformation isn't about improving; it's about rethinking and unapologetically showing up for life.

Success for God looks like being thirsty for his presence, repentance, and radical obedience. Praise him without strings attached. Do not question him. Once you get a revelation of God's glory, love, mercy, grace, long-suffering, and readiness to forgive, the Holy Spirit will continually open your eyes to more aspects of his nature and character. You'll have an ever-increasing revelation of God in the way he wants to be known to you.

Let the revelation of God's glory become so real to you that you become rooted and grounded in it. Develop this unshakeable trust as you keep seeking it, studying it, claiming it, and appropriating it in your life until the vision of Christ's glory bursts forth in you. As you remain in the Word and seek the revelation of his glory, you'll be changed and keep changing from glory to glory.

Belief and desire are the keys to being transformed by God. The Holy Spirit eagerly waits to supply faith and the grace needed for its operation: "Therefore I say to you, whatever things you ask when you pray, believe that you receive them, and you will have them" (Mark 11:24 NKJV). Here, Jesus gave us four keys to being fruitful in our calling.

1. Desire means to beg.
2. Pray means to communicate with the Lord.
3. Believe means to put one's trust in.
4. Have means come to pass or it will be.

When we have an attitude of expectancy and crave something godly, we eagerly desire to spend time with God and receive it from him. But before God can do what he wants to do in our lives, we must fix whatever is hindering our lives and blocking what God has for us. We cannot move forward in his promises unless we release what's holding us back whether it's a bitter heart or anger. He cannot fill a vessel that is already filled.

When we are emptied of bitterness and anger, we'll be ready to be blessed to do God's work. We must check our hearts for what is not of God and allow him to fill us instead with his promises. Bearing fruit is the result of living in Christ and Christ living in us, so hindrances are all the things that prevent this. Here are some possible hindrances.

- unwillingness to accept truth and grow in the Word (study Pss. 111:10, 16:11; 1 Chron. 16:11)
- mind-sets—sin focus, condemnation, shame, unworthiness, anxiety, control (study Phil. 2:5, 4:8, 4:6–7; 2 Cor. 10:5)
- attitudes—bitterness, unforgiveness, resentment, anger (study James 4:10; Phil. 2:3–5; Eph. 4:32, 4:31; Heb. 12:15; Rom. 12:10; 1 Tim. 6:10)
- unwholesome talk—slander, gossip (study Prov. 4:23–24; Eph. 4:29)

- being lukewarm or cold to the things of God (study Rev. 3:16)

God gives us gifts and talents for us to steward, but he is most interested in the character we steward. It doesn't take a seasoned gardener to know that good and bad seeds look alike when they are in seed form. Only after extensive education and experience can a farmer recognize a seed for what it truly is. The same is true when we consider the attitudes of our hearts: "For as he thinks in his heart, so is he. As one who reckons, he says to you, eat and drink, yet his heart is not with you [but is grudging the cost]" (Prov. 23:7 AMP).

If we're not careful, bad-seed attitudes can take root in our hearts and eventually sprout into dangerous weeds of wrong behaviors. Some seed attitudes may seem appropriate on the surface, but after deeper introspection, we see that the motives behind these attitudes dishonor God: "Above all else, guard your heart, for everything you do flows from it" (Prov. 4:23 NIV).

Every word, deed, and attitude starts with a thought we choose to think. If we have bad attitudes or habits, we've probably allowed seeds to sprout roots. By checking our hearts regularly, we are better able to deal with situations before root problems become entangled in the expression of our personalities and performance. We can "study to shew thyself approved unto God, a workman that needeth not to be ashamed, rightly dividing the word of truth" (2 Tim. 2:15 KJV). Our character is the foundation for everything we do with God, so we must be diligent to guard out witness.

The Bible says, "If we confess our sins, he is faithful and just to forgive us our sins and to cleanse us from all unrighteousness" (1 John 1:9 ESV). When we become aware of any bad seeds expressed in our thoughts, attitudes, or emotions, we can quickly repent and allow God to pull them out. As we open our hearts and extend our faith, we will receive the grace to overcome. Many times, God will not expose our issues publicly but will bring us into times of inactivity so he can plow our souls until all the unhealthy roots are removed and replaced with his attributes.

If we want to spur one another on toward love and good deeds, we have to start with ourselves (Heb. 10:24). Sometimes, the best way to throw off everything that hinders us and the sin that so easily besets us is to focus all our energy on putting on something new. If we compare the biblical characters of Joseph and Jacob, we can see who was diligent about being transformed and putting on God's garments and who was not.

Joseph	Jacob
Joseph is open to hear from God (Gen. 37:5).	Jacobs tests God's leading (Gen. 47:9).
Joseph believes in divine providence (Gen. 45:5–8, 50:20).	Jacob counts all things against him (Gen. 42:36).
Joseph's testimony reveals a life of challenges and victories.	Jacob's testimony reveals a life of resistance and conflict.
No matter what came against Joseph, he determined to keep God's perspective and maintain a selfless spirit.	Whatever came against Jacob, he constantly tries to outwit, manipulate, or survive it to prosper.

It's not so much what we go through in life but our spirits and attitudes that determine the outcome of our lives and testimony. We can choose whom we model our lives after—we can look more like Joseph in diligently following Jesus, or we can look like Jacob in resisting him. Personal transformation will take place in our lives when we identify specifically what God wants us to change.

We must not be vague if we want to make progress. The Holy Spirit will faithfully convict us and provide us a clear understanding of exactly what we should take off and put on in our lives. Like hindrances, the things to put off are sinful habits, patterns, and tendencies that God wants us to change. The put ons are habits and patterns God wants us to be, do, or become.

Put Off the Old Man	Put On the New Man
(Relevant scriptures to meditate on are in the NIV.)	
anger (Prov. 29:22)	self-control (Gal. 5:22–23)
bitterness (Heb. 12:15)	tenderheartedness (Eph. 4:32)
boasting (1 Cor. 4:7)	humility (Phil. 2:3)
criticism (Gal. 5:15)	kindness (Col. 3:12)
discontentment (Heb. 13:5)	contentment (1 Tim. 6:8)
disobedience (1 Sam. 12:15)	obedience (Deut. 11:27)
complaining (Phil. 2:14–16)	gratitude (Gal. 5:22–23)
jealousy (Gal. 5:26)	trust (1 Cor. 13:4)
people pleasing (Prov. 29:25)	fear of God (Luke 12:4–5)
unbelief (Heb. 3:12)	faith (Heb. 11:1)
dirty clothes (Gen. 35:2)	new garments (Isa. 61:10)
discouragement (2 Cor. 4:8–9)	full armor (Eph. 6:10–18)

If you feel overwhelmed, never forget this truth: "For it is God who works in you, both to will and to work for his good pleasure" (Phil. 2:13 ESV).

As we consecrate ourselves, the sanctifying and co-laboring will occur naturally over our lifetimes; it is not a quick-fix strategy but a lifelong process of renewal and restoration. Self-denial is the secret: "Then Jesus said to his disciples, 'Whoever wants to be my disciples must deny themselves and take up their cross and follow me'" (Matt. 16:24 NIV).

God doesn't call us to work more, pray more, or do more; he calls us to himself, and real, authentic love comes when it's called. God is pleased when we believe in his son, Jesus, and he is not pleased when we do not. God is not impressed with our good and benevolent works if we have no faith in Jesus. If we believe and trust in God, he is impressed.

Though we have had experiences with God, many of us still struggle with trust and faith. We forget that "the Spirit gives life; the flesh counts for nothing. The words I have spoken to you-they are full of the Spirit and life" (John 6:63 NIV). Our physical bodies give us hunger pangs, and our spiritual bodies are hungry to spend time with God and in his Word so we don't fight battles we weren't called to fight.

> Stop toiling and doing and producing for the food that perishes and decomposes [in the using], but strive and work and produce rather for the [lasting] food which endures [continually] unto life eternal; the Son of Man will give (furnish) you that, for God the Father has authorized and certified Him and put His seal of endorsement upon Him. (John 6:27 AMP)

God expects us to commune with him continuously and drink of the Living Water, the Holy Spirit, so we will be filled by him. We can enjoy everything through the Holy Spirit's power. He will provide peace and joy we should not let the enemy steal.

Jesus asked us, "Did I not tell you and promise you that if you would believe and rely on Me, you would see the glory of God?" (John 11:40 AMP). Jesus knew we would have many things vying for our attention and wanted us to cleave to him so his example of living would become natural to us despite what we were surrounded by. He said,

> Walk according as ye have the light, Walk as men who are conscious that the light is among them, use your opportunities; do not ask questions to raise objections, but ask them in order that you may know the truth. (John 12:35 AMP)

As we walk in the light of God's Word, the Holy Spirit works with us to bring our minds to new levels of truth awareness.

Entering these new levels means leaving the old ones behind and trusting God to mature us with new revelations. God knows we need help understanding his plan for us; if we trust his Spirit, we'll live the abundant lives God wants us to have. Paul wrote,

> For it is by grace [God's remarkable compassion and favor drawing you to Christ] that you have been saved [actually delivered from judgment and given eternal life] through faith. And this [salvation] is not of yourselves [not through your own effort], but it is the [undeserved, gracious] gift of God; not because of [your] works [nor your attempts to keep the Law], so that no one will [be able to] boast *or* take credit in any way [for his salvation]. For we are His workmanship

> [his own master work, a work of art], created in Christ Jesus [reborn from above—spiritually transformed, renewed, ready to be used] for good works, which God prepared [for us] beforehand [taking paths which he set], so that we would walk in them [living the good life which he prearranged and made ready for us]. (Eph. 2:8–11 AMP)

As we entrust ourselves to him, he reveals his plans to us. God uses his power to do his will through is, so we need to cooperate with him and dare to stretch to new realms in him. We must refuse to have a secondhand relationship with him; we must seek to know him closely for ourselves. He calls us to his glory and excellence; he wants us to have excellent lives. He expects us to behave excellently and avoid whatever would compromise our spending time with and developing with him.

Only Jesus has the power to finish what he started; the Bible says we should fix "our eyes on Jesus, the pioneer and perfecter of faith. For the joy set before him he endured the cross, scorning its shame, and sat down at the right hand of the throne of God" (Heb. 12:12 NIV). Jesus completes and perfects everything he starts, and that includes us.

We can't expect Jesus to work in us if we don't trust and depend on his operation. Jesus came to earth to be our example of how to rely on the Father and his Spirit. We're responsible for meeting and coming into agreement with him; we have access to unlimited power when we're determined to remain plugged in.

We must learn how wonderful we are in God and how helpless we are in ourselves. Without his power operating in our lives, we can do nothing. Jesus is deeply invested in our lives weaving the good, bad, and ugly together for his glory and purposes and our good, but we must welcome and allow his success in us: "I no longer live, but Christ lives in me. The life I now live in the body, I live by faith in the Son of God, who loved me and gave himself for me" (Gal. 2:20 NIV).

If we accept the call to follow Jesus, we must be ready and willing to be salt and light and commit to the transformative work of the Holy Spirit in and through us. This process does not come easily, and it assuredly does not come without a fight.

Will you fight the good fight with the pioneer and perfecter of your faith?

PROMPT FOR REFLECTION

Are you walking worthy of the call to a consecrated life?

PRAYER

Lord, I thank you that you have called me with a holy calling not according to my works but according to your purpose and grace, which was given me in Christ Jesus. "He has saved us and called us to a holy life-not because of anything we have done but because of his own purpose and grace. This grace was given us in Christ Jesus before the beginning of time" (2 Tim. 1:9 NIV).

I know that you plan existed for me before I knew you and that you will bring it to pass. Help me walk in a way that is worthy of my calling. "As a prisoner for the LORD, then, I urge you to live a life worthy of the calling you have received" (Eph. 4:1 NIV).

I know you have an appointed plan for me, and I have a destiny that will be fulfilled.

Chapter 3

The Fight

But we are not of those who shrink back and are destroyed,
but of those who have faith and preserve their souls.
—Hebrews 10:39 (ESV)

Faith enables us to live above our senses. Our faith must not be a private thing; it ought to be the most public thing about us. Living by faith rather than by sight enables us to see God's glory.

"Fight the good fight of the faith. Take hold of the eternal life to which you were called when you made your good confession in the presence of many witnesses, then you also know that faith is a fight" (1 Tim. 6:12 NIV). We must fight to keep our faith stirred up, and we have to view faith as one of our greatest weapons. Without faith, we can't please God and we can't battle our enemy effectively. If we really want God in our lives, we must determine to put him in them so he won't have to fight for a spot: "Commit everything you do to the Lord. Trust him, and he will help you" (Ps. 37:5 NLT).

Sometimes, life is extremely hard, painful, and heartbreaking. Sometimes, we go through circumstances that are relentlessly difficult, and we think our circumstances are unchanging for a long time. When life is relentlessly tough, we have an opportunity to discover how relentless God is. In my struggles, I've discovered how relentlessly kind he is, how relentlessly gracious his is, how relentlessly merciful he is, and how loving and beautiful his nature is.

Rest is a weapon. Maybe you're familiar with this scripture.

> Come to Me, all who are weary and heavy laden, and I will give you rest. Take My yoke upon you and learn from Me, for I am gentle and humble in heart, and you will find rest for your souls. For My yoke is easy, and My burden is light.

It's important that we experience the rest of partnership with God. We are invited to lives without fear, anxiety, worry, or panic. We are invited to lives in which we never need to react to something because our lives are geared to respond to someone.

The power of denial is the power of not accepting what doesn't match the Word of God or God's best for your life. Whatever it is, you won't acknowledge it, let it have power over you, or come into agreement with it. You know God is supernatural and can supersede anything in the natural.

On the flip side, you do have to be careful of the kind of denial that can keep you stuck and has the reverse effect on your life. I'm reminded of Elisha and the Shunammite woman from 2 Kings. The Shunammite woman struggled to receive a prophetic word from the Lord through the prophet Elisha. The prophet told her, "'Next year at this time you will be holding a son in your arms!' 'No, my lord!' she cried. 'O man of God, don't deceive me and get my hopes up like that'" (2 Kings 4:16

NLT). Her strong denial was working against her; she knew God was the real deal, but despite that and what had been manifested for others around her, she was reluctant to stand on God as her solid ground.

This can be true for us too. Sometimes, it's easier for us to believe what we've wanted for so long is simply not going to happen or is not for us especially if we know only lack or in the Shunammite woman's case barrenness. However, denial isn't protection. We must be careful about what we say or resist, about what inner narratives we tell ourselves just to stay safe especially when Jesus is in the equation. There is nothing too hard for God. We can't afford to deny our blessings just because we're scared; we have to believe.

The Shunammite woman did not conceive at the appointed time as Elisha prophesied. What's interesting here is that just as soon as she conceived her son, he died, and she cried out to Elisha, "'Did I ask you for a son, my lord?' she said. 'Didn't I tell you, "Don't raise my hopes"'?" (2 Kings 4:28 NIV). Talk about spiritual warfare. Don't think the enemy won't come at you as you receive what you've been praying for. Remember, "The thief comes only to steal and kill and destroy; I have come that they may have life, and have it to the full" (John 10:10 NIV).

Despite her words to Elisha, the Shunammite woman had said "it is well" when asked about her son by a man named Gehazi on her way to Elisha. This is important; that time, despite her hurt, she knew what the enemy was up to, so she took a different approach. She refused to agree with what she saw and empowered herself with the truth.

When you're empowered, you're strong. You're bold enough to believe God, and the enemy can't stand against you. When you have adverse circumstances in your face, remember that the devil is a liar. He will bring up old pains to tempt you to think it's real, but unless you come into agreement with his lies, they can't happen. What can you do instead? Get into a Shunammite mode; refuse to doubt God's promises with supernatural denial. Say, "All is well" and challenge yourself to take authority over any lie, fear, doubt, or tormenting spirit trying to shake your faith.

Spiritual warfare is real; it's imperative that we keep our appointments with the King and fight to stay mentally present. Some energy won't leave without a fight. Where we feel weak, we should lean in and the Lord will give us supernatural peace during whatever we face. As we choose to depend on him and submit to him, we will see him fight our battles and situations resolve themselves. "Submit yourselves, then, to God. Resist the devil, and he will flee from you" (James 4:7 NIV).

Like the Shunammite woman, commit to where you are going and stay focused. This may also mean being vigilant about getting distractors and doubters out of your atmosphere. You may have to evict the naysayers and those who don't believe miracles happen and who question what you're believing for. Only Elisha could enter the room where the Shunammite woman's son was because he knew he couldn't afford to have any negative energy impact his impartation, and sure enough, the boy was made whole by the spiritual perfection of God.

God tells us he will be with us as we go through water and fire. We will have to face some tests and trials; they cannot be avoided. They are intended to strengthen us and develop our character, make us persevere, sanctify and purify us, teach the unique lessons of suffering and the benefits and disciplines of sacrifice, and make us better persons.

We often cringe when we think about these things, but if we want to become all God created us to be, our characters will have to be prepared to get through our trials. When we face difficulties, we must realize God is using them to strengthen and change us or advance his purpose for our lives. The fruit of godly character must be developed, and very rarely does that occur when things are going along as we want. We are wise to settle down and deal head-on with the challenges he puts before us. Whatever they are, if we will receive them as his training for us and submit to his will, we will not get stuck; we will get through them and get to greater glory and victory. The sons and daughters who are being forged in the fire will come forth radiating the manifested character and glory of God.

Prayer is real, powerful, and effective, so don't let others convince you otherwise. They have obviously never experienced the power of prayer in their lives or are oblivious to the impact others' prayers for them have had on them. That's unfortunate because prayer is incredibly effective. You can worry or you can trust in God. Trusting in God will change everything, but worrying will make things only worse. Provision is believing you possess all you need to do what God has called you to do.

Being stewards of the baton of faith in our generation can seem like a lot of responsibility, but God entrusted us with the gospel. We don't need to see what we can do; we just need to be convinced of what God can do. We are to collaborate with God; that is our new measure of safety and success, and that makes everything a destiny decision. How well are we partnering with him? Anything God is in has hope in it, so it will be impossible for us to be bored. If we're breathing, that means the best is yet to come.

You have been given gift of the Holy Spirit, and he is evidence that you have been anointed for whatever assignment he has for you. He wants to elevate you and take you somewhere. You are a carrier of God's glory. You are his fingerprint on the world, and you have the greatest impact when you submit to God's positioning system.

Our partnership and co-laboring with the Holy Spirit today is our greatest measure of success and impact. Jesus knew we would have difficulty fixing our eyes on him and encounter our weaknesses; he said, "My grace is all you need. My power works best in weakness. So now I am glad to boast about my weaknesses, so that the power of Christ can work through me" (2 Cor. 12:9 NLT).

Faith is the heart of your spiritual life; the enemy wants to choke it out of your life. Just as heart failure tragically affects the body, a failure of faith can make your spiritual life helpless. The good news is that God has given you a measure of faith, and as the Thessalonians demonstrated, your faith can grow exceedingly and keep you from reacting to the lies of the devil. You can stay with your measure of faith or keep growing it.

God is waiting on you and the currency of your faith. God is no respecter of persons; he is a respecter of faith: "God hath dealt to every man the measure of faith" (Rom. 12:3 KJV). When you start saying things that are beyond you even if you don't believe them, you begin singing the song of the highest version of yourself and align with that truth; suddenly, you are saying and becoming all God wants you to say and become.

Here's the real deal—God wants to get the glory from your life. Listen to Jesus's words "Come to me." This is an invitation to embrace Jesus's nature; this is wonderful news for you in this season. It has to do with how you live. You can refuse to carry the weight of the world on your shoulders and exchange it for rest, his easy yoke, and then learn from him. Draw close to him and he'll give you something. Every time you link up with God, he will balance you out. His grace allows you to be at rest, powerful, and in authority when the world would have you be otherwise.

Sometimes, God needs to know if you can rest. If you can get into position, if you're convinced of all he promised you, things can come at you but you'll live in a place of rest that will bring you into the next dimension. You don't win battles with emotion; you win in rest. You size up the problem, rehearse God's promise, and rest while he shows up. In this wisdom, you'll learn that you can't keep a snake from biting you but that you don't have to absorb its poison. God will take care of your enemies too if you learn how to rest.

Your forced rhythm and manner of hustling outside the Spirit's leading can be an idol that leads to addictive habits and rebellion. It puts you at war with God. It's either God's way or your way. You win when you realize God can do it better than you can. It makes you powerless. Give up the idol of your rhythm and "learn the unforced rhythms of grace" (Matt. 11:28–30 MSG). As Matthew so eloquently wrote,

> Are you tired? Worn out? Burned out on religion? Come to me. Get away with me and you'll recover your life. I'll show you how to take a real rest. Walk with me and work with me—watch how I do it. Learn the unforced rhythms of grace. I won't lay anything heavy or ill-fitting on you. Keep company with me and you'll learn to live freely and lightly. (Matt. 11:28–30 MSG)

Can I get an amen! Staying at rest is your best battle strategy. Rest says,

I have learned to be content whatever the circumstances. I know what it is to be in need, and I know what it is to have plenty. I have learned the secret of being content in any and every situation, whether well fed or hungry, whether living in plenty or in want. I can do all things through him who gives me strength. (Phil. 4:11–13 NIV)

God is most impressed by what we do under pressure, not what we say we'll do. What if we learned to relax during warfare? We should enjoy where God has us now and know he is bringing us through something. It's one thing to go through a crisis grandly but another to go through every day glorifying God when there are no witnesses or limelight. The test of life is not success but faithfulness in life as it naturally is.

The power of rest gives us the way forward. It takes more faith when we're accustomed to always be on the go. Where busyness is celebrated, it's difficult to realize that being busy is a weakness. It's an excuse to avoid what's hard and uncomfortable. It has become normal to accept all things swirling around and living under the weight of constantly having to create. There is a rhythm to that lifestyle, and we can pattern ourselves after it to the point that we don't know how to rest well. Work withdrawals have become an interesting phenomenon; we buy into the lie that if we take it down a notch and drop the pace, we won't be able to come back up to the rhythm we supposedly need to be successful. So we change our temperaments.

Many say that progress doesn't just happen, that we have to fight and press in to lay hold of what God has for us. This is not a new revelation, but rest is a powerful form of progress too even though it often doesn't feel very productive. Power is not explosions and physical exertion; instead, the most powerful position to be in is rest. Power is being whole enough and convinced enough and having faith enough to rest in the Lord's covering. Being an empty instrument ready for God to use is the greatest joy. Through alignment and anointing, he sets us on track to pursue the vision and purpose he has for us.

Early in my spiritual walk, I thought that when people were saved and started being intentional about living for the Lord, that would make them exempt from battles. But the more I lived this new life and walked salvation out, the more I recognized that battles come no matter what side of the fence you're on.

Even if you're living in your own way and in your own strength, you'll still have struggles and heartbreaks. But after you start co-laboring with Christ, you will have his protection in the battles you face; whatever you face won't kill you.

If we aren't careful, we will try to battle spiritual warfare the same way we fought before and not understanding that because we follow Jesus, some battles are par for the course. We cannot engage in spiritual warfare the same way we fought before we became spiritual. When we are resting in God, fighting looks different: "Be still, and know that I am God; I will be exalted among the nations, I will be exalted in the earth" (Ps. 46:10 NIV). We are still and know God is on the throne. We are still and know God is with and for us.

You can fight without moving at all. Your presence, your confidence about who has gone ahead of you and what you've been called to do enables you to not say a word and still be engaged in battle. Angels are around you and navigating on your behalf so much so that you can sense what's really a battle and what's not. You don't have to launch out into the battle and start wailing because you know how to fight and be still.

Sometimes, breakthroughs don't come until you cry out to God. But what's even more difficult than crying out to God when you're in a battle you have no business being in is when you're in a battle God brings to you. You can be doing things the right way, making the right decisions and suddenly a battle comes to you. When you do things the right way, it doesn't save you from battles; it actually attracts them. When battle comes to you, you have a decision to make, and instead of crying out to God, you have to trust him.

Trusting God is sometimes harder than crying out to him. If you've disobeyed God, you understand why the only choice you have is to cry out to God for mercy and help, but when battle comes to you, it makes you wonder if you're doing things the right way, it makes you wonder if you're qualified to be doing what you're doing, and it makes you question yourself. Right before the battle, you were fine. You knew you were doing the right things and were proud of yourself, but then you can't understand why if all was going so well a struggle came to you. You have to trust God though you feel you've been ambushed.

When we are in these battles, we have to remember who God is. Sometimes, the only way to be still in the fight is to remember who put you in the battle and that you're not in it on your own. Sometimes, we need to get in our prayer closet and make a demand on God. We decide not get off of our knees until God sends us a word. We need God to show us who we're becoming due to being under attack; we want to know what God is trying to show us. In 2 Chronicles, Jehoshaphat waited to hear from God.

> Listen, all you of Judah and you inhabitants of Jerusalem, and you, King Jehoshaphat! Thus

says the Lord to you: "Do not be afraid nor dismayed because of this great multitude, for the battle is not yours, but God's." (2 Chron. 20:15 NKJV)

God wanted King Jehoshaphat to know the battle was not over him. We also may be in battles, but not all battles are about us. If we don't understand this, we'll start asking, "Why is this happening to me?" Some battles are about what God wants to do in us. We tend to make things about us and about what we've done wrong or what we could do better. When we understand that the battle is about something he is doing in us, we derive a confidence and assurance. The more we make it about ourselves, the more we're guaranteed to lose we are nothing and can do no good thing on our own.

When you recognize the battle is about what God is doing in you, when your role in battle is to see how God can increase in you, he becomes greater than anything around you. Your role in battle shifts from defending yourself to allowing God to increase by what he is doing in you.

Despite our disobedience and wrong decisions, God sometimes wants us to know that a battle we're in is the result of what he is doing in us. The battle is part of our process; we figure out who God is and recognize what he has placed in us. This kind of battle is not ours but God's. Angels are backing us up, a hedge of protection is around us, and all things will work for our good. Because we know who God is and have partnered with him, we can be stirred up when the enemy tries to tear us down. When God magnifies himself in us, we will rise and push the darkness away. When we engage in battle, it can't be about us. The Holy Spirit, who allowed Jesus to rise from the dead, is in us magnifying our strength.

God laid this foundation for Jehoshaphat because he wants us to know the battle is his especially when it doesn't look like it is. If the battle isn't ours, does that mean we don't have to fight? You know the answer. The battle isn't ours, but we still have to stand up to it. The Spirit of the Lord is a bit confrontational. We are guaranteed the win, yes, but God will not allow us to ignore the attacks when we have the power to end them.

Jehoshaphat and his men were told this.

> You will not have to fight this battle. Take up your positions; stand firm and see the deliverance the LORD will give you, Judah and Jerusalem. Do not be afraid; do not be discouraged. Go out to face them tomorrow, and the LORD will be with you. (2 Chron. 20:17 NIV)

Sometimes, God wants us to position ourselves and stand still because he wants us to see he is on our side. He lets us show up to battles with grace, class, and dignity and with the confidence that in the middle of an attack on our hearts, our position is still one of praise and worship to God. We are not threatened; we are so connected to the Spirit that we give God permission to have authority over us. United like that, we set an ambush for everything trying to ambush us. We remember who we are and get our fight back.

God will have you preserve energy in battles that aren't yours so you can reap the rewards and not be tired out fighting battles that don't have anything to do with you. Be still and know that God is on your side and that your worship is releasing ambushes. When the battle is over, the treasure God has placed in you will be your reward.

Believe it or not, we're still fighting when we're praising. It doesn't look like it, but we are getting in a position to keep our hearts right so God can still use us. We can trust him when battle is breaking out all around us. The best way to fight is not controlling the narrative of our lives but being still and living in a posture of worship and praise that allows us to fight. This is the right kind of fight. It doesn't need validation; it just needs to hear from God. Being still protects what God has placed in us. Being in relationship with God gives us the power to stand up to our life battles.

Sometimes, battling is prophesying and speaking out against the enemy's lies. Death and life are in the power of the tongue, and those who love it will eat its fruit. We can choose to allow what we say to bring life and speak blessings. We can choose to steer our lives into blessings by filling the atmosphere around us with words of faith and victory. We cannot have faith without speaking it. The way of the world and the law is about doing, but faith is about speaking: "It is written: 'I believed; therefore I have spoken.' Since we have that same spirit of faith, we also believe and therefore speak" (2 Cor. 4:13 NIV). We believe; therefore, we speak.

As you guard your mouth, consider these points.

1. Command your morning. Speak the Word of God over your day. His divine order expressed through you will bring freedom to you. Rise up early to receive insights, instructions, or even warnings from the Lord. Learn to love and delight in the empowerment he provides before you even step out of your house.

2. Guard your first response. The enemy often wants to stir up fear in us through our circumstances and people

in our world. Rather than reacting to what you see, practice confessing your righteousness, not fear. Go into the Shunammite mode.

3. Grow in righteousness consciousness. Eat the Word daily to strengthen your spiritual walk. Meditate and apply the Word to your life so your thoughts will align with God's. If the truth is not established in your heart, start speaking it. This isn't to be confused with worrying about trying to have enough faith.

Look to Jesus, and use his faith. Don't worry about trying to be transformed. You can't change yourself by your own power. Apart from God, you are nothing. Don't worry about not having enough either; just look to Jesus. How do you know when you really trust God in the battle? A rest will take over—God will begin doing the heavy lifting and take you to levels you couldn't have accessed on your own.

Faith can be difficult because it's easier to be a spectator than a participator. Theodore Roosevelt made this seem so simple in one of his famous speeches.

> It is not the critic who counts; not the man who points out how the strong man stumbles, or where the doer of deeds could have done them better. The credit belongs to the man who is actually in the arena, whose face is marred by dust and sweat and blood; who strives valiantly; who errs, who comes short again and again, because there is no effort without error and shortcoming; but who does actually strive to do the deeds; who knows great enthusiasms, the great devotions; who spends himself in a

> worthy cause; who at the best knows in the end the triumph of high achievement, and who at the worst, if he fails, at least fails while daring greatly, so that his place shall never be with those cold and timid souls who neither know victory nor defeat.

Hebrews reminds us Jesus is the role model we can count on to be the "man in the arena."

> Therefore, since we are surrounded by so great a cloud of witnesses [who by faith have testified to the truth of God's absolute faithfulness], stripping off every unnecessary weight and the sin which so easily *and* cleverly entangles us, let us run with endurance *and* active persistence the race that is set before us, [looking away from all that will distract us and] focusing our eyes on Jesus, who is the Author and Perfecter of faith [the first incentive for our belief and the One who brings our faith to maturity], who for the joy [of accomplishing the goal] set before Him endured the cross, disregarding the shame, and sat down at the right hand of the throne of God [revealing his deity, his authority, and the completion of his work]. Just consider *and* meditate on Him who endured from sinners such bitter hostility against Himself [consider it all in comparison with your trials], so that you will not grow weary and lose heart. (Heb. 12:1–4 AMP)

We need to remember this encouragement. We are surrounded by a great crowd of witnesses who have fought the good fight of faith before us and made a way for us. The baton of faith has been given to us to be faithful witnesses to this generation. This is our time; there is no plan B. We are the answer we've been praying for. Will we stir up our faith and fan our flames enough to believe it?

Because Jesus went through everything we could ever encounter, we don't have to squirm when life gets tough. Focusing on Jesus will help us remain fixed whether things on the outside seem to be going well or falling apart. Joy and suffering are different parts of the process of sanctification, but as we train ourselves to endure, we can keep the light in us alive. If we have any light at all, it is for God's glory. By ourselves, we are flickering inconsistencies, but as disruptions in our souls occur and we submit our wills to God's authority, he fans our flames.

In Revelation, the church in Ephesus was encouraged to repent for having abandoned God in their faith walk so he could get them back on track: "Yet I hold this against you: You have forsaken the love you had at first" (Rev. 2:4 NIV). The Spirit and the truth will lead and guide our hearts and minds when we abide in the Spirit. If we are drifting, we need to repent and turn back to God. God's eyes aren't going to and fro looking for perfectionists in the faith; he is looking for those whose hearts are right and pure before him and who continue to treasure him above all else.

Faith alone is not enough to fulfill destiny. When we're going through troubles, we must resist the temptation to grow weary or lose heart. If the enemy can wear us down, he will dominate us, but if we resist, we can win. This calls for endurance in spiritual warfare. Unfortunately, we can't download endurance, but we can build it. Endurance is built through resistance and through pressure, our favorites.

> Patient endurance is what you need now, so that you will continue to do God's will. Then you will receive all that he has promised. And if you needed another boost, By your patient endurance, you will gain your souls. (Luke 21:10 NIV)

Will you go in and possess your spiritual Promised Land?

The measure of the trials I faced directly relates to the hope I can give the world. That doesn't sound lovely when you first hear it, but when it gets into your spirit, you realize that means surrendering. When we embrace what God allows in our lives and move through it, we realize if we've given all we know of ourselves to all we know of God.

In Acts, Paul and Silas exemplified great faith; they settled in their souls that Jesus was who he said he was. While in prison, they could have focused on so many things, but they responded to their circumstances with worship.

> About midnight Paul and Silas were praying and singing hymns to God, and the other prisoners were listening to them. Suddenly there was such a violent earthquake that the foundations of the prison were shaken. (Acts 16:25–26 NIV)

These men believed "God is a spirit, and his worshippers must worship in Spirit and in truth" (John 4:24 NIV). When their wills were crossed, they knew to depend on the Spirit, abide in God, and remain settled in his truth. They sang hymns and praises because they'd have been miserable without worship.

The apostle Paul said this about faith.

> For this reason I bow my knees before the Father, from whom every family in heaven and on earth is named, that according to the riches of his glory he may grant you to be strengthened with power through his Spirit in your inner being, so that Christ may dwell in your hearts through faith—that you, being rooted and grounded in love, may have strength to comprehend with all the saints what is the breadth and length and height and depth, and to know the love of Christ that surpasses knowledge, that you may be filled with all the fullness of God.

Paul encouraged Timothy not to let the flame of faith burn out: "For this reason I remind you to fan into flame the gift of God, which is in you through the laying on of my hands" (1 Tim. 1:6 NIV).

What in your life threatens to extinguish your flame? What pushes the darkness in on you and diminishes your awareness of God's presence? For many, it is doubting God's existence. Doubt is the culprit behind this generation's complacency. It looks like half-heartedness or being lukewarm. God despises this spiritual state: "But since you are like lukewarm water, neither hot nor cold, I will spit you out of my mouth" (Rev. 3:16 NLV).

James told us our supernatural God wants to perform supernatural works through our belief and willingness.

> If any of you lacks wisdom [to guide him through a decision or circumstance], he is to ask of [our benevolent] God, who gives to

everyone generously and without rebuke *or* blame, and it will be given to him. But he must ask [for wisdom] in faith, without doubting [God's willingness to help], for the one who doubts is like a billowing surge of the sea that is blown about and tossed by the wind. (James 1:5–6 AMP)

How we fight our doubt can build our faith. The more we believe in the supernatural power to change our minds, the more we can resist doubt. Paul told Timothy his faith would overcome the world and keep his life ablaze.

When we build lives that need God, we stir up a holy fire in our souls that enables us to fight sin, overcome temptation, and live in the world as ambassadors for Christ. Good disciples practice daily disciplines and recenter their hearts on God alongside others who keep them accountable. It's important to live with other faith-filed believers because we can falsely believe certain things are disqualifying us and we need others' encouragement to see that we need God the most. Power, love, and self-control are our portion. These create the right barriers around our faith so it can flow in and through us.

Paul made faith practical for Timothy because he knew he wouldn't always be able to see what he needed to see, and Paul didn't want him to be tempted to be defined by his disappointments. Paul reminded Timothy of a few ways to fan his flame.

He reminded him of who he was in Christ. Knowing who we are protects us from many attacks against our identity. When we know who we are in Christ, we can afford to stand firm through uncomfortable situations that would otherwise make us flinch or compromise.

He reminded him of God's call and his gospel, the good news. He reminded him that his faith, not fear, motivated and empowered him. He encouraged him to stay motivated by faith alone and guard against being consumed and driven by fear.

He reminded him of what is worth holding onto and guarding, and he inspired him to reengage. We are often tempted to shut down or isolate ourselves when the going gets tough, but Paul encouraged Timothy to fan the flame of all God had put in him rather than focusing on distractions.

He reminded him of what he needed to release to press on into destiny. We can't allow our worries, expectations, unhealthy appetites, or anything that weakens us to knock us down. We've been invited to run a unique race, but we will never run well and with endurance if we are weighed down by things we've outgrown or were never meant to carry.

A good visual for what it looks and feels like to be willing to surrender in faith is trapeze artists. A trapeze artist swings and gains the right momentum to release herself from the swing and be grabbed by her catcher. If you let go of whatever you fear letting go of, will you trust God to catch you? Your acceptance of the call means that you say yes to God and fearlessly abandon anything that doesn't work toward his ends.

We need mothers and fathers who will raise up the younger generation. We need people who believe they are called and qualified for discipleship. These godly relationships provide nurturing, discipline, instruction, belonging, and identity. Those who went before us left their mantles, passed their batons of the roles and responsibilities to us, and we must take their batons and keep running. We fix our eyes on Jesus, the greatest man in history. He had no servants, yet he was called master. He had no degree, yet he was called teacher. He had no medicine, yet he was called healer. He had no army, yet kings feared him. He won no military battles, yet he conquered the world. He committed no crime, yet he was crucified. He was buried, yet he lives today.

If Jesus is in us, we can go where we couldn't have gone on our own and carry the batons we have received. With God, we can preach the gospel, demonstrate the kingdom, and manifest his glory throughout the earth.

A biblical example is the story of Elijah and Elisha. When Elijah ascended to heaven in a whirlwind, he left his whole mantle to Elisha. When Jesus ascended to heaven, he gave us his mantle in portions according to our abilities. This is why it says that when he ascended on high, he took many captives and gave gifts to his people. What does "he ascended" mean except that he also descended to the lower, earthly regions? He who descended is the one who ascended higher than all the heavens to fill the whole universe.

> So Christ himself gave the apostles, the prophets, the evangelists, the pastors and teachers, to equip his people for works of service, so that the body of Christ may be built up until we all reach unity in the faith and in the knowledge of the Son of God and become mature, attaining to the whole measure of the fullness of Christ. (Eph. 4:8–13 NIV)

We should build our lives on the foundation of our faith if we want to disciple well. If we let the Spirit come alive in us, we will find that the value of hearing revelation from God is beyond measure. We all have a natural desire to know what God has to say to us personally. God created us to need vision. When God's Word is declared over a matter, it puts creative force into being to help accomplish his will in that situation. When combined with faith and spiritual warfare, this allows his divine purposes that could never have occurred in the natural realm alone to come into being. Running the race is about perseverance and endurance; it is staying the course as an effective witness of Christ.

Will you pay the price to allow God to develop your gifts so you can influence communities, the marketplace, and churches so you can make a difference? God looks for those who are willing to sacrifice their comfort, battle opposition, and lead others to freedom. You can have an effect on culture and the social order by God's Word and power; this is how the world will be changed, but it starts with you. As you challenge yourself to change, you will challenge others to do likewise. You're called to build, equip, lead, reform, battle, or perform miracles; such kingdom exploits are needed for our times. God wants to use you and your testimony to bring breakthrough.

To walk out our faith and fulfill the call, we need to work together. An example of this comes from Samuel. Though Eli didn't hear the Lord, he knew how to guide Samuel to respond. Good mentorship teaches us how to respond well to life. Sometimes, God disturbs our rest and disrupts our peace to get our attention. With the help of mentors, even if we don't know the Lord or aren't as experienced in walking out our call, we can come to know God through our service to him.

Samuel's job was to keep the light burning in the temple of the Lord. Though he didn't know the Lord, he discovered him through serving him. The Lord called Samuel: "And he ran to Eli and said, 'Here I am; you called me.' But Eli said, 'I did not call; go back and lie down.' So he went and lay down" (1 Sam. 3:5 NIV). Samuel did not yet know the Lord or his Word, but Eli perceived that the Lord had called the child. So Eli told

Samuel, "Go and lie down, and if he calls you, say, 'Speak, LORD, for your servant is listening.' So Samuel went and lay down in his place" (1 Sam. 3:9 NIV). Samuel honored God without even fully knowing him. Eli knew God and had such an intimate relationship with him that he was not perplexed at Samuel having heard the Lord's voice. Under Eli's mentoring and submission to the Lord, Samuel grew to be one of the greatest prophets of the Lord.

When you're walking by faith, you're walking without seeing where you're going. If you've ever done a trust fall—you fall into the arms of someone standing behind you—you have a sense of the discomfort. It's a challenge to walk out what God has called you to do. You have to know God is leading you even when everything around you is changing. The enemy attacks you because he hopes you don't find out and realize who you are.

Sometimes, we try to disqualify ourselves from the call of God and wonder how he can use us; I've failed too much and struggled too much. But be encouraged; God's not looking for what's popular; he's looking for who's faithful.

Sometimes, we wish we didn't need God as much so we could work instead and prove we can do things, but we're all in need of Jesus's covering and grace. The best place we can be is in a state of helpless and in need of our Savior's mercy and grace and realize we can produce nothing of value without him. We need to show effort before God does his part. Being faithful doesn't mean being perfect; it means when we fall, we get up and keep going. God wants to see us thrive; he wants to be able to tell us, "Well done." To hear this, we have to do a few things well that others simply will not do at all. It's okay to struggle, but it's not okay to play with God's holiness.

What if people are waiting for you to get into position? Who might be tied to your obedience? You are called to impact what's around you because you are heaven's seasoning. Wherever God has planted you is where he intends you to be. Change can be very uncomfortable, and warfare can seem intolerable at times. However, you have the choice to stay in your comfort zone or become more like Jesus. If you are a faithful steward, you will rule and reign with Christ.

Before moving into these life areas, take some time to revisit your vision. What do victory, abundance, breakthrough, overflow, vindication, and favor look like? These all sound like things we should desire and pray for, but they're often beyond what we've planned or have achieved for ourselves. We all have to ask God to align us with the destiny and path he has for us; no path will look the same. We want only what's ours. Look at each area on the wheel with Jesus at the center.

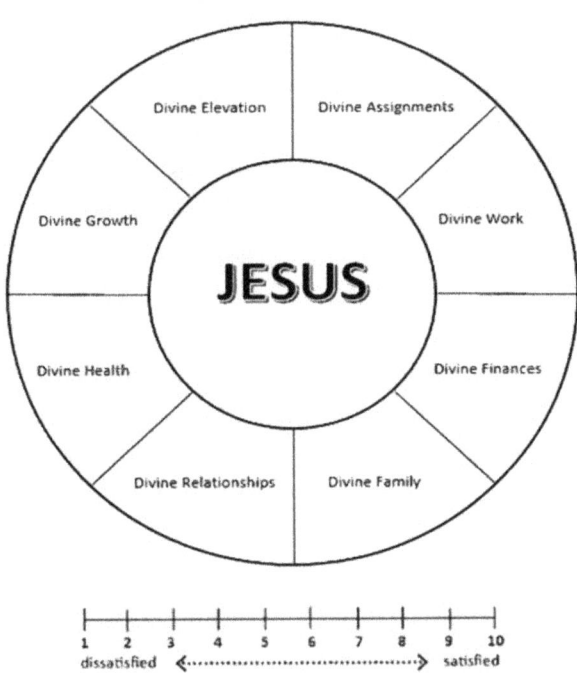

Are you willing to hear his voice and obey his Word in each area of your life? Will you be bold and stir up your faith? Will you stand for God's promises when the enemy attacks what God has revealed to you? This is the fight of faith. If you are called to be an ambassador of God's freedom to a hurting world, you must first come into a new place of freedom for yourself. Will you do the Word to sharpen your gifts of revelation and vision?

As you move forward, pay attention to how you can release the power of God's voice in everyday situations as well as your different life experiences and challenges. In each area, God challenges you to get into position, and as you do, your witness will inspire others to partner with God and your testimony will help equip them. Stir up your faith and cross over to possess your inheritance: "For those who are evil will be destroyed, but those who hope in the LORD will inherit the land" (Jer. 9:24 NIV).

Future generations will be blessed by your choice to obey God. The Lord will use you to impact and bless others. He is raising up anointed influencers equipped to enter territories, regions, cities, and industries and bring with them the message of Jesus Christ even as they relate in relevant ways to this current generation.

Are you one of them? They speak a unique language. They carry signature glory. Their arrival shifts atmospheres and impacts culture. They are anointed influencers sanctioned and sent by God. The Lord will use them to affect and bless others. If this is you, get ready for growth and establishment to come into your life as you step into this assignment.

We are to live in God's glory daily. God has designed us to create success and abundance in all our spheres of influence. We must keep making choices to press on even when we don't see an immediate return.

PROMPT FOR REFLECTION

In what areas of your life is it difficult to receive blessings from God?

PRAYER

Lord, make me continually aware that my greatest need will always be for more of you in my life. Don't let me get to the place where I think I can live my own life without you. Help me recognize my complete dependence on you. I crave your presence, peace, power, and perfect love. I want to walk so closely with you that I hear the Holy Spirit speaking to my heart at all times.

I submit my needs to you. Increase my faith. I lift up to you my heart's longings and desires and recognize that you are the source of and answer to everything I need or long for. Thank you for supplying all my needs and ordering my steps according to your perfect will.

Chapter 4

Divine Assignments

> Now the Lord says to me, "It isn't enough for you to be merely my servant. You must do more than lead back survivors from the tribes of Israel. I have placed you here as a light for other nations; you must take my saving power to everyone on earth."
> —Isaiah 49:6 (KJV)

God will often interfere with your plans and interrupt your life, and that is the greatest test of your obedience. He will ask you to sacrifice something you love. You are on an assignment; the world depends on you just as the salvation of the world depended on Mary carrying out her assignment.

You know you're surrendered and committed to your assignment when you're tempted to murmur and complain, doubt, worry fear, return to the old, shift your disposition, or let social media dictate your steps. Don't fall for that. Think instead of what God will do because of what you see, and shift the flow of what could have been worry to worship. Speak the exact opposite about your life as if it's about to happen in a spirit of thanksgiving, and offer the sacrifice of worship.

It can be wise to enlist in spiritual coaching and bring someone on you team who can help you stay focused and accountable to moving forward and prophesying truth. Don't get impatient, and watch your heart's attitude through tests and trials. God is in control, so relax and let him direct your steps. You'll want to run from some places, and if you're not reading your Bible, you won't receive conviction that you're there for a purpose. Greatness can be unlocked only by chaos. Something has to break for greatness to unleash itself. In spite of what happens, be determined to enjoy your life and praise your way from pit to palace.

Perhaps one of the best examples we have of purpose is Mary. She taught us by going through her own process how God's will is done. Mary did what we are all to do—deliver something to the earth from God. Everything God does gives us a principle for life. For example, God plants a seed that becomes a tree that bears fruit, but he follows certain principles for that to happen.

As Mary did, we are to follow God's patterns; if we do, we will succeed. I would rather follow God than anyone else and even myself. His methods must be excellent because he always succeeds. We are wise to imitate him and model our ways after his. God is so sure of his success that he wrote the end of the story before the beginning.

In the incarnation story, we learn how to follow God's strategy to bring about what God wants.

- Conceive. Spend quiet time with God to listen and hear what he has next for you. "He changes times and seasons; he deposes kings and raises up others. He gives wisdom to the wise and knowledge to the discerning" (Dan. 2:21 NIV). This verse provides clarity that God

controls the events of your life and is willing to give you the wisdom and knowledge to walk in his mysteries.
- Believe. When you know in your heart that God has called you to your next adventure, let nothing convince you otherwise. Satan will try his best to distract you and create chaos in your life, but don't focus on that or you will be tempted to give up. You have to persevere by being so convinced that what God told you is the only thing that matters and that God will have the final say. All you have been through has prepared you for what you are going through. Follow the Holy Spirit's leadership; he will lead you all the way through.
- Protect. Many times, you may think you just need to pray more, read the Bible more, or worship more, and yes, that will strengthen your spiritual walk, but God also requires practical action to protect the word he's given you. Are there practical changes you need to make in your life for the place you know God is taking you? If he gave you what you've been praying for today, would you be ready? Are you attached to anything that could prevent you from moving forward? Evaluate what has to be changed in your surroundings and make those changes.
- Deliver it. Never quit. You will have opposition to overcome. Find a spiritual mentor to help you move to the next level. Surround yourself with your intercessory team to pray with you, and call on them when you're in need. Accept that God chose you for this assignment, and take bold and courageous steps of faith. "As the body without the spirit is dead, so faith without deeds is dead" (James 2:26 NIV). God is faithful: "He who began a good work in you will be faithful to complete

it" (Phil. 1:6 NIV). Decide you're finally going to fully go for it with him.

Spiritual assignments don't always come neatly packaged. Sometimes, we may ask God for success and he provides an opportunity to work in a place that allows us to develop physical and mental stamina. We may plead for prosperity, but we may receive a broader perspective on how he views prosperity and an opportunity to increase our patience. Other times, we may petition him for growth and are blessed with the gift of grace.

God provides what we need for our spiritual development and gives us spiritual assignments that strengthen our confidence so we will pursue what is worthy of him. Spiritual assignments often change with different spiritual seasons in our lives. No matter the season, focus on becoming more like Christ. When God says you've been in a place long enough, it's time to move. You went through everything you did in the past season for your benefit and to prepare for the promotion God has for you in this season. Your tests and trials will be your triumph going into your next assignment. Jesus is turning everything around for you. How you handle the tests and trials will determine your increase.

When you are set on winning and moving forward, you may notice that the familiar begins chasing you and trying to pull you back. In these times, it's important that you get this seed rooted into your spirit: "And he shall be like a tree planted by the rivers of water, that bringeth forth his fruit in his season; his leaf also shall not wither; and whatsoever he doeth shall prosper" (Ps. 1:3 KJV). And Jesus said, "I am the vine, ye are the branches: He that abideth in me, and I in him, the same bringeth forth much fruit: for without me ye can do nothing" (John 15:5 KJV).

If you are guided by the Holy Spirit, your assignment no matter where you find yourself is to practice the fruit of self-control to get your thoughts, words, and emotions under his authority, to get the garden of your soul together and position yourself properly so you can flourish.

Just as you eliminate weeds from your garden quickly and with precision, demand excellence of everyone connected to you. I've noticed particularly at the beginning of a new year once all of the hype and inspiring words have been stirred up, the new year seems so mediocre. I look around and wonder, *Did I really step into anything new?* In this moment, you decide to continue business as usual or raise your standard of what you will accept as normal. Something will likely nudge your spirit to let you know that to get to the things of God, you'll have to raise the bar and hold yourself and those around you accountable to a higher level of excellence. Excellence is not a trend or fad; it's purely God.

> Then this Daniel became distinguished above all the other presidents and satraps, because an excellent spirit was in him. And the king planned to set him over the whole kingdom. (Dan. 6:3 ESV)

> Finally, brothers, whatever is true, whatever is honorable, whatever is just, whatever is pure, whatever is lovely, whatever is commendable, if there is any excellence, if there is anything worthy of praise, think about these things. (Phil. 4:8 NIV)

Show yourself in all respects to be a model of good works, and in your teaching show integrity, dignity. (Tit. 2:7 NIV)

But as you excel in everything—in faith, in speech, in knowledge, in all earnestness, and in our love for you—see that you excel in this act of grace also. (2 Cor. 8:7 NIV)

His divine power has granted to us all things that pertain to life and godliness, through the knowledge of him who called us to his own glory and excellence, by which he has granted to us his precious and very great promises, so that through them you may become partakers of the divine nature, having escaped from the corruption that is in the world because of sinful desire. (2 Peter 1:3–4 NIV)

I love when God spoke to me about vibes because he was telling me excellence has a rhythm and it's about attracting equally. He knew I could understand this, and he was prompting me to become more aware of the way he operated and to study his character so I could know him and know what I carry.

Until you recognize these truths for yourself, you will be susceptible to many paradigms and ways of living. God was helping me understand my assignment and carry an excellent spirit. God was prompting me to ask myself, *Am I excellent?* Would you do business with someone you felt was less than excellent? If you identify with excellence, you will find it increasingly easier to not stand for less. This is not a haughty attitude but an honor for whom God has called you to be and what he has given you to steward. Not tolerating mediocrity is not arrogance; God didn't call you to stop on your journey; he called you to reach the top and keep reaching. Your team is everything, so choose them wisely.

I learned through exploring my spiritual assignment to be excellent that excellence begins as a mind-set and that as you grow in it, you are to excel in your acts of grace. Excellence looks like God. You sacrifice your growth when you lower your standards to appease others. You need to encourage people to strive for excellence, and you can do that by modeling excellence based on the Word. Place a demand on yourself. You don't have to wait for some new thing to shift or show up; you can be the shift and begin functioning in a new paradigm.

How you start an assignment is a good predictor of how you'll finish it. Many start a new year with fasting and prayer, spending quiet time reflecting or setting new goals, and visioning; you can get in the habit of starting each day in worship, meditation, and prayer that will give you stability and consistency. Worship will help position you so you'll know what to pray for. Often, you start your day praying, but these prayers can be more routine than heartfelt or they can be just about your needs; you are seeking God's hand rather than his face. Worship cuts through all that so your heart can connect with God's heart and the Spirit can lead you in what to pray.

Worship is the secret place. "Whoever dwells in the shelter of the Most High will rest in the shadow of the Almighty" (Ps. 91:1 NIV). You can worship even in the middle of a busy day by stopping and praising God. I was convicted on this when the Lord asked me, *Are you giving me your best?*

Proverbs 3:9 tells us to give the Lord the first of our produce. That led me to ask what I was giving the best of myself to. What was more important than my relationship with

God? Journal entries like this are humbling, but they always bring me back to the truth.

David had mastered worship: "O God, You are my God; Early will I seek You; My soul thirsts for You; My flesh longs for you In a dry and thirst land where there is no water" (Ps. 63:1 NKJV). "My voice You shall hear in the morning, O Lord; In the morning I will direct it to You and I will look up" (Ps. 5:2 NKJV). David was determined to speak to God.

Start each day in worship, meditation, and prayer. Your plans for the day may change. Especially if you are lacking clarity on God's will, fasting will increase your sensory experience of him. You plan your ways, but it is really God who establishes your comings and goings. Sometimes, you will have things on your calendar but will come out of prayer and worship time and readjust your plan.

The only way you can guarantee success is if you know God is ordering your steps, so remind yourself and God that you belong to him. Asking God if your plans are in alignment with his plans for you will keep you from playing God in your life. You want to remain in alignment with his will so you can be the tree planted by the Living Water. Be still. Put your agenda and vision on hold. Allow God to either confirm or redirect your day.

Meditation is a bit different; it is rehearsing what God has said to you. Average churchgoers go to church and hear God speak to them words of confirmation and validation and even correction, but that happens to them only in church. If faith comes by hearing the Word of God, how many times do you need to hear something before it becomes real for you?

When God gives you a word, it's not to make you feel good in the moment; it's to make you one with that word so you can see it take place in your life. This comes by meditating on the word. In the morning, journal about and rehearse what you have heard. God has given you a word, so speak it over and over to yourself. Remember that God spoke and it came to be. His Word does not return void; it is on you to relate to his Word until it is produced in your life. You want to be fully convinced of what he has said.

Once worship and meditation have happened, then you pray and pray, "Let it be manifest." Never underestimate the power of what God can drop in your spirit in your time of worship and meditation. One word, one idea, one thought, one game-changing revelation can radically transform your life. After your morning practice, you will manage your life easier. There will always be more demands on your energy than you can handle, so stay filled up with what God provides and allocate your focus and time wisely.

God gave you your first breath, and before you leave this earth, you will take your last breath, so your breaths are limited as is your energy. God has given you only enough to fulfill your purpose, so make up your mind to regulate it.

Everything outside of you is after your energy, time, and focus. Think of it like a bank account; if you don't manage it properly, if you respond just because there is a demand, you won't have the energy or resources you need for what really matters. That's why I love this verse: "All you need to say is simply 'Yes' or 'No'; anything beyond this comes from the evil one" (Matt. 5:37 NIV). Whether you like it or not, not everything can have all of you, and you have to be the one who says no, one of the most powerful words. Be intentional about where you invest yourself.

When you're pursuing God and walking out your spiritual assignment, you may not see progress, but keep coming and all at once it will appear. At the beginning of something, we are fired up and ready for open doors, but as time passes, we experience resistance. We should encourage ourselves in the Lord. God shows us something, but it takes longer than a minute for it to manifest. Let us not become weary. We serve a suddenly God. At times, we feel a disconnect between what's around us and what's in us, and if we're not careful, we can become jealous, angry, and bitter. When our surroundings and social media aren't adding up and we start comparing ourselves to others, we can start to doubt God. But God does the right thing at the right time. Don't believe this makes you ordinary or you aren't special; keep going. When your season is due, it will spring forth. Focus on what God is developing. You are progressing on the inside, and that it the ultimate assignment. The seeds you have planted will bear a harvest.

Your assignment is to invest yourself wisely and not accept mediocrity. Everything in your life has to line up with the vision God has shown you or it will no longer be good enough. "Do you not know that those who run in a race all run, but one receives the prize? Run in such a way that you may obtain it" (1 Cor. 9:24–26 NIV).

You are no longer random; you've been spending time with God, and you have a clear vision about where things ought to go. Fight against every thought of inadequacy. In time, your preparation will accelerate. When you are living your life in preparation, seeking the Lord, abstaining from sin, and obeying his voice and Word, he will seem to reward you suddenly; he is not playing games with you. Suddenly, all that you have sown will bear fruit.

God will tell us to shift when he needs us to see life through a different lens. It is our responsibility to be so rightly related to him that we don't miss or misinterpret his promptings. Looking at life through a different lens gives us humility for others' processes. We will have grace for other people because we're looking from where they were sitting. God wants us to stay in position and focused on him so when he blesses us, our response will be, "Thank you! Who am I supposed to bless?"

When God breathes on what you've been sowing, will you be ready? Your assignment is to keep him first no matter where he positions you or how he blesses you. If you live right, you will accelerate people in their purposes as well. If God gives you power, it will be for his purpose, not yours. He wants you to lead with weakness and humility and never believe you are greater or lesser than anyone else but believe that without him, you'd be nothing. God opens and closes doors.

Walking with the Holy Spirit will keep you acquainted with the things of God. He will ignite your purpose and give you the grace to focus on your assignment. You want to move in step with him because if you rely on yourself, your flesh will let you down; and if you count solely on your talent and abilities, you won't fully mature, but your spirit will if your character allows it. As you pursue your assignment, the enemy will look for you where he last saw you, but as you mature, you will step out on the word God has given you and will not be in the same place. God knows what you need to push the purpose in you out of you.

Satan will do the best he can to distract you from your assignment, and that is when you will need to speak life and get out of your comfort zone. Whatever has your name on it is for you. Your life is moving at the speed of your assignment; recognize whatever is slowing you down and trust God to help you make adjustments. Put on the full armor of God. He has called you to walk in wealthy places, and your benefits are about to kick in.

PROMPT FOR REFLECTION

What assignment does God have you focused on? What is he prompting you to do to be more effective in your assignment?

PRAYER

May peace settle into my soul as I wait on the Lord. May joy rise up in me at a moment I least expect it. May provision come out of nowhere and remind me that God has my back and he goes before me. May I defy the odds and come back from the trials I've endured. May I thrive right here in the place God has me. And may my life be a living, breathing testimony of God's grace, goodness, kindness, and love. I matter so much to him.

CHAPTER 5

Divine Work

> Whatever you do, work at it with all of your
> heart, as working for the Lord, not for men.
> —Colossians 3:23 (NIV)

When you co-labor with Jesus, your work focus shifts from what the world may consider work. Your work does not fit into a nine-to-five schedule necessarily; it has much more to do with who you are and who you are becoming.

Two people live in you. Hear me out. One is confident, powerful, and secure, and the other is weak, prideful, and insecure. Most of the time, you get along fine, but when the right person comes along, the pull of the other you is just right and what you didn't want to happen happens. It's the battle between your flesh and your spirit, your carnal and your new, redeemed nature.

> This means that anyone who belongs to Christ
> has become a new person. The old life is gone;
> a new life has begun! And all of this is a gift
> from God, who brought us back to himself

through Christ. And God has given us this task of reconciling people to him. (2 Cor. 5:17–18 NLT)

This means you are to celebrate that the old has passed away and all things have become new. The unfortunate thing is that the old man will constantly try to resurface.

An example of this is the kind, wonderful Peter who walked with Jesus and the other Peter who spoke a curse. "Jesus turned and said to Peter, 'Get behind me, Satan! You are a stumbling block to me; you do not have in mind the concerns of God, but merely human concerns'" (Matt. 16:23 NIV). The other you is in all of us. We have proof of this: "If you live according to the flesh you will die; but if by the Spirit you put to death the misdeeds of the body, you will live. For those who are led by the Spirit of God are the children of God" (Rom. 8:13–14 NIV).

Living by the flesh could be living for a dream, potential, relationship, feelings, or grudges that compromise your walk in the Spirit and prevent you from getting where you're supposed to be. Your work is to keep that nature dead and resist giving into the temptation to be drawn back into your old ways. When you decide not to be ruled by your flesh, you'll do the right thing even if it's uncomfortable. Right things could be studying for a test, not speaking back when you're offended, and growing. It takes discipline, and no discipline feels good at the time, but later, it produces righteousness. The key is being consistent.

You'll never become so spiritual that you don't have to deal with carnal desires. Like the apostle Paul said, the old man dies daily. Every day, you have to say no to things. Your old man is not that strong, and you can choose not to feed him. Every time you give into temptation, get offended, or lose your tempter, you are feeding the negative and engaging the old man.

Starve the negative and it will become weaker. God is bigger than any temptation or stronghold, and he created you to be free of them. David had to defeat his personal enemies before God could trust him with his Goliath. He could have slacked off, but he was a person of excellence. Because he was faithful in defeating his personal enemies, God promoted him. The Lord wants to move you into position.

So what does it mean to succeed in this type of work? For you personally, it may mean fine-tuning what you're running after with this one life. What do you consider your great work? You may struggle with that question because you could consider many things, but what does success look like to you? When you don't understand what it is, you become uninterested in it or make up what the win is.

I've studied the Word and begun to picture what I think Jesus wants personally for you and for me as believers, and it's found in the book of Matthew. Some context here: after Jesus was resurrected, he spent forty days on earth to heal and talk to his disciples and prepare them for what he would do after he ascended. This is the last conversation he had with his disciples; he told them to do something for him: "Therefore, go and make disciples of all the nations, baptizing them in the name of the Father and the Son and the Holy Spirit. Teach these new disciples to obey all the commands I have given you" (Matt. 28:19 NLT).

What would you do if these were your last words of instruction from you most treasured leader? You are to be a disciple and make disciples, personal followers of Jesus. This is a personal responsibility. A disciple learns from Jesus and learns to live like him. So a disciple building disciples—that's the win. Is that your win?

What does that even mean? It's good to battle with this because God has a verse for this too: "When you produce much fruit, you are my true disciples. This brings great glory to my Father" (John 15:8 NLT). Interesting. God gets glory when you bear much fruit, when you make disciples. This is your playbook from now on. If you've ever asked yourself, *What is my work? What am I supposed to do with my life?* the answer is to become a disciple and make disciples. You do that by bearing much fruit.

In what areas in your life are you fruitful? There may be a lot of areas where you are and others where you are not. To bear the fruit of the Spirit means that whoever looks at your life sees that you're carrying good fruit such as the fruit of love that prompts you to love even those who don't love you. The world gets to see the fruit of Jesus in your life. John wrote, "Your love for one another will prove to the world that you are my disciples" (John 13:35 NLT). God wants the world to know you're his disciple, and the world will know that by the fruit you bear.

Another reason you carry fruit is so people can eat it. When you carry fruit in your life at the store, at school, at work, and at home, people will come to eat it. When people meet you, they should be able to taste and see that the Lord is good. There is nothing like being around people who are positive, who are bearing fruit, who nourish you. This is proof that you are a real disciple. Wherever you work, God wants fruit. It doesn't matter if you feel fruitful or if you feel you are being very fruitful, God wants to produce more fruit in your life. You will transform when you carefully consider your fruit.

INNER FRUIT—FRUITS OF THE SPIRIT

You've heard about the kind of fruit that is developed in you. The Holy Spirit is working things into your character and moving other things out. Like a detox, a good cleansing of the wrong things in your system makes way for the right things to be integrated. This kind of fruit looks like love, joy, peace, patience, kindness, goodness, faithfulness, gentleness, and self-control. "But the Holy Spirit produces this kind of fruit in our lives: love, joy, peace, patience, kindness, goodness, faithfulness, gentleness, and self-control. There is no law against these things" (Gal. 5:22–23 NLT).

OUTER FRUIT—GOOD WORKS

This kind of fruit has to do with what the world sees: "Let your light shine before men in such a way that they may see your good works, and glorify your Father who in in heaven" (Matt. 5:16 NLT). As the fruits of the Spirit start working in you, they mature, and what you produce on the outside from this process are actions that model Christlikeness.

PEOPLE FRUIT—SOUL WINNING

This is not about invading personal space but about engaging people intentionally knowing that hell and heaven are real and God has given you a mandate. He wants fruit in your life so you care enough about other people to get outside your comfort zone, insecurities, and personality and touch others: "The fruit of the righteous is a tree of life, and he who wins souls is wise" (Prov. 11:30 NLT). When you are always looking for occasions to share Jesus's love and grace with others, God says you're a wise person. Are you wise?

The most wonderful thing about the Bible is that it gives you clarity on how to balance your life. All your work will depend on one word, *desire*. "For God is working in you, giving you the desire and the power to do what pleases him" (Phil. 2:13 NLT). God is so good that when he starts working in you, he gives you a new heart and the desire and power to do what's required to produce the fruit of the Spirit. That's divine work because we on our own cannot produce this fruit consistently in our own strength or by our willpower.

God wants you to be fruitful; the only thing you have to do is be willing to be used by him. The part you don't like is the pruning, but the only way God can get you to the place of more fruit is to cut things off from your life that would stunt your growth. Some of the things you think you are walking through are a punishment when really you're just being pruned. Pruning is painful, relocating is painful, and having to do without some things in your life that have been crutches for you is painful. But God desires and sees more for you.

Divine work is about changing your perspective. Often, this happens in seasons that seem very difficult when the Holy Spirit isn't speaking to you. You're frustrated and losing sleep, but the Holy Spirit can use what you consider a horrible situation to qualify you for something great. God must work on your attitude, self-control, and patience so he can produce more fruit through you.

Will you see abiding as your divine work? Will you get so locked into God that he can get to you anything he wants that will produce fruit in your life? Abide means to stay in one place for a long time. You can't do that if you're moody and have little patience. God wants you to stay with him through your struggles.

If you run every time you get offended, every time you feel overlooked, or every time things aren't working in your favor as far as you can tell, you'll miss the opportunities to bear much fruit. You've probably heard that the best-tasting grapes are those that have endured the struggle. If you stay committed to God and endure the struggle, you will produce much fruit. It's hard to stay put, but what might God be producing while you stay faithful?

Fruit is all about the root. If you stay connected to God, your life will be supplied for. Apart from God, nothing divine can be produced in your life. Your attempts will be futile if you aren't connected to the root. If you just stay connected to God, you will produce much fruit. When you are with God, "You can do everything through Christ, who gives you strength" (Phil. 4:13 NLT). There is no work more important than remaining connected to God and being fruitful.

Divine work often comes with lessons and learning opportunities. I was once told by a wise friend that these were learning opportunities, my favorite. As it turned out, that was the case for me. After running a nonprofit for nearly three years, it was time for my formal review. I woke up during fourth watch, got prayed up, texted for support from my intercessory team, and read about Daniel and his spirit of excellence. It was no coincidence that God led me to study early that morning; God is not random. Feeling fired up, I even had some solid worship going on; I was singing all about how God was fighting for me and pushing back the darkness. I was ready, and so was my boss.

The most wild and careless words started spewing out of her mouth the moment she arrived on the scene. She was not prepared for my review, and she made it her heart's delight to speak down, bully, and try anything within her power to get a reaction out of me. As I listened, I felt I was surrounded by a bubble that none of her fiery darts could burst. I wasn't identifying with or absorbing any of what she was spitting. I knew who I was really working for, the quality of the work I'd put, in and the spirit I'd consistently shown up with, so I was not about to cave in. God supplied me with his grace to respond out of my renewed nature rather than emotion, fear, or insecurity. Advancement happened that day.

Don't get me wrong; it's a big disappointment when your prayers don't look like your reality. How could anyone sit through that humiliation and workplace bullying without asking, *God, where are you?* My encouragement was to keep battling in the Spirit, keep praying, and keep believing until God showed up. It took time, but my boss ended up giving me a promotion, shared scripture with me, and asked for prayer. That was miraculous. We were graced with a few long conversations during which I was able speak my truth and move forward into a new position with new hope and less drama, pettiness, and chaos.

Sometimes, the best often comes out of the worst situations. Usually, this is accurate except when you are set on being the worst at the expense of others. If it weren't for my desire to see change and my belief in a better world and the vision of what the organization I'd invested in was doing, I'm sure my emotions and frustrations would have had me walking out the door, but I turned to God and pressed on.

> But the Lord is with me as a mighty terrible One; therefore, my persecutors will stumble, and they will not overcome (me). They will be utterly put to share, for they will not deal wisely or prosper (in their schemes); their eternal dishonor will never be forgotten. (Jer. 20:11 AMP)

> Kings will be your foster fathers, and their queens your nursing mothers. They will bow down before you with their faces to the ground; they will lick the dust at your feet. Then you will know that I am the LORD; those who hope in me will not be disappointed. (Isa. 49:23 NIV)

Learn to love the struggle as much as the reward. So many people want to get to the peak but hate climbing. They want success but not the struggle. People want to grow, but they don't want to go through any growing pains. You'll eventually transition from being skipped over to being sought after if you keep the faith and work the vision.

My work taught me to pray boldly and believe big. You are destined to achieve your success in Christ. Also, what a setup! The Lord let me know that he was about to bless me in such a way that I'd have no doubt whatsoever that it was he who had done that. He is a big God who does things in a big way. Unlike me at times, he doesn't think small, plan small, or execute small decisions. We laugh at the phrase "If you want to make God laugh, tell him your plans" because it's so true. We can try to control every detail of our lives, but the only thing that impacts us is our experience of life. If we had the whole plan, we wouldn't need God. He shows up in big, bold ways that we can't imagine.

PROMPT FOR REFLECTION

Have you asked God what work he wants you to do? Have you committed all your work to him?

PRAYER

Lord, I pray that you show me what work I am supposed to be doing. If it is something other than what I am doing now, reveal that to me. If it is something I am to do in addition to what I'm doing, show me that too. Whatever you call me to do, I pray you will give me the energy and strength to get it done well.

Enable me to do what I do successfully. May I find great fulfillment and satisfaction in every aspect of it, even the most difficult and unpleasant parts. Establish me and the works of my hands so what I do will find favor with others and be a blessing for many. May it always be glorifying to you.

Chapter 6

Divine Finances

> Whoever loves money never has enough;
> whoever loves wealth is never satisfied with
> their income. This too is meaningless.
> —Ecclesiastes 5:10 (NIV)

I hope you're sensing a pattern even if it seems impractical when it comes to the most powerful thing you can do to co-labor with God: keep your eyes on Jesus. It's so easy to doubt or forget the Lord is personally interested in making you a success in your life.

Inevitably, when your mind is set on the favor of the Lord, you will begin to experience like never before a confident expectation of good regardless of the adversity or challenge thrown in your way. God says, "But seek ye first the kingdom of God, and his righteousness; and all these things shall be added unto you" (Matt. 6:33 KJV). Your human tendency is to depend on your own strengths to succeed, but divine finances are finances you've put in God's hand.

God is committed to doing everything to make sure you have more than enough resources to fulfill your purpose. If you've been frustrated or flustered when it comes to your finances, you're not alone. But if you obey God and submit to what he is doing, submit your priorities to his, and submit to his stewardship training, you will come into his favor. "Let the Lord be magnified who takes pleasure in the prosperity of his servant" (Ps. 35:27 NIV).

God wants you to believe in the impossible. Maybe there are practical reasons you haven't achieved what you consider financial success. Have you been meditating on Jesus? "Keep this Book of the Law always on your lips; meditate on it day and night, so that you may be careful to do everything written in it. Then you will be prosperous and successful" (Josh. 1:8 NIV).

Let's say you've made your first million, but when you examine your life, your struggle to make more money has also created some costly losses of the things you once thought were more important. This is not the divine working in your finances. When God blesses you with financial well-being, that's only a small part of his favor on your life. The success he brings will not take you away from his priorities for you; they will lead to greater fulfillment in all areas of your life. God is your good success. Do you believe that "the Lord owns the cattle on a thousand hills?" That the Spirit of God is able to breathe on your finances and do suddenly what you tried to do for years? He doesn't want to do this for your personal pleasure and enjoyment but to push you further into his purposes and plans than you could go on your own. God will prosper you in your finances so you can achieve the ends he's anointed you for.

Your crying out in stress and fear or doubting God's integrity because of your finances doesn't bring God glory. He has been providing for his people since time began. Have you ever considered that you've been anointed for an uncommon purpose to do uncommon things? Whatever God has called you to, he is obligated to provide for you.

Focus you heart on what God is doing in your life. Your financial status is not your source. If you are stressed, vexed, and bummed out because you're not making enough money, you're distracted. But you can focus on your purpose, what God has planned for you. You don't have time to be vexed about a job.

The greater and stronger your grip on your purpose is, the more you will receive promotion, elevation, and opportunity that will finance what God has called you to do and be. Don't settle for life as it is or as you see it; believe in God and catch up with his will for you to prosper. What one step has he nudged you to take that is the key to your next level? Maybe it's getting more knowledge, hiring a financial advisor, or creating and sticking to a budget. God will not leave you without good, orderly direction. Make time for him so you can hear his direction for you. There is no reason the Holy Spirit cannot move you toward the prosperity that is yours. What is his vision for how you can use his power in your finances? Divine finances are about purpose. For your potential breakthrough in this area, let go of the status quo.

> God blessed them and said to them, "Be fruitful and increase in number; fill the earth and subdue it. Rule over the fish in the sea and the birds in the sky and over every living creature that moves on the ground." (Gen. 1:28 NIV)

I see a blessing system in this verse. God commands fours things: be fruitful, multiply, replenish, and subdue. God wants you to always be producing, increasing, and controlling your environment. God does not want you to be stagnant, in debt, or stuck in poor spending patterns. He wants you to learn, grow, get organized, and develop a new financial mind-set. Do you think God has a higher quality of life for you? Will you accept what you've seen, or are you willing to stretch and do what he requires?

You shall have what you say. That's not new age; that's the Bible: "Therefore, I tell you, whatever you ask for in prayer, believe that you have received it, and it shall be yours" (Mark 11:24 NIV). Abraham was a man of faith I admire; he was revolutionary. He spoke as if the promise God had spoken to him in Genesis had come to pass. To me, a logical, organized, recovering perfectionist and people-pleaser, this is one of the most uncomfortable yet wise things you can do with your creative energy. Speak the truth and only the truth. Speak it so much that you are annoyed by your own voice. Let the promise get all the way in you until you start to believe it before it even happens. It starts with your words. Do you believe the divine can move in your finances? Enough that you will speak it?

Don't second-guess God. Fear will make you stop doing what you're meant to do, run your life, and change your direction. I learned the hard way that your fear will always be wrestling with the hows and whys and lead you straight into mental exhaustion, but your faith takes God at his word. Fear causes a ripple effect of bad choices you can't afford. Remember the Spirit you have been given: "For the Spirit God gave us does not make us timid, but gives us power, love and self-discipline" (2 Tim. 1:7 NIV). Claim these words and know your Father loves you. If you let him, he will change your fear to faith and you'll see a shift in your reality.

Real faith is sharing responsibility and collaborating with God. Matthew's parable of the three servants offers us a clearer understanding of the stewards God wants us to be. You have good and profitable or wicked and unprofitable choices. God will entrust you with whatever he pleases, but only when you are faithful with what he has given you will he give you more.

In this parable, the first two servants traded their talents, and their master said, "Well done, good and faithful servant! You have been faithful with a few things; I will put you in charge of many things. Come and share your master's happiness" (Matt. 25:21 NIV). The other servant was afraid and had buried his talent. His master said, "Thou wicked and slothful servant, thou oughtest therefore to have put my money to the exchangers, and then I should have received mine own with usury" (Matt. 25:30 KJV). This servant wasn't interested in increasing or profiting; he had hindered his prosperity by burying what he had been given. God wants you to put your resources to good use. Are you faithful with what you've been given? Excelling in your purpose and finances requires godly wisdom.

Your finances are not evil, but what you do with your finances can be. Healthy finances give you options. The Bible says money gives you "an answer for all things," but it can become an idol in your life: "A feast is made for laughter, wine makes life merry, and money is the answer for everything" (Eccl. 10:19 KJV). You can easily turn your income into an idol, but you can keep that from happening if you grow in tithing and keep God first.

Satan comes when God blesses you. As you near the place God has for you, your Garden of Eden, the tempter will come to convince you out of the place, so remain alert and diligent with your finances. Be careful whom you let bless you, and be aware that you ought to turn down some blessings, those that aren't divine. If they're not from God, you don't want them.

Do you have the courage to be blessed financially? Maybe you've heard, "To whom much is given, much is required," and that intimidated you.

> But the one who does not know and does things deserving punishment will be beaten with few blows. From everyone who has been given much, much will be demanded; and from the one who has been entrusted with much, much more will be asked. (Luke 12:48 NIV)

Is it because you think you will sabotage your success? Who told you that? People can enable your poverty by their mentality. Stop doing whatever keeps you from being blessed. "Fear not" means it takes courage to be blessed. Blessed is not a look; it's a reality with your priorities in place. You'll get darts shot at you when you're successful; you have to be tough to be blessed. Do you have faith that God has your back? Is your mentality in shape? Are your emotions in check? Is your house in order? There's no limit to how much God will reward you, but a blessing when you're not ready for it can feel more like a curse.

Start thinking generationally and about your successors—children, mentees, and others. Whom do you want to catch the overflow? Think like God. Position yourself. Perhaps no one gave to you in such a way so you're not thinking generationally, but forward-thinking people position themselves to be blessed. You must live in this moment but think in the next. If you don't prepare for the next moment, you'll forfeit the vision. What's next? Who's worthy of it?

God has something in mind for you; he has plans for you to win in the end, but he can't dispense it until you obey him. It's not about you; you are prospered so you can prosper the world around you. If you want to thrive and be salt and light in the world, you need to practically organize your finances.

God wants to give wealth to those who have the wisdom to move the kingdom forward. Gain is not godliness. You can be rich, evil, and suicidal. But godliness with contentment is great profit. God looks at motives. The more stuff you have, the more you're under stress, pressure, and temptation and the target of enemies and haters. More means more. Can you stand what you're asking God for?

If you follow your purpose, profit will follow you. There is balance to this. You have to need it without loving it, and you have to constantly check yourself on this. Check the covetousness spirit. You do not want anything that God doesn't have for you. Hate comes from covetousness, so break that off you. You can't fight the devil in someone else's armor; you can win only in your armor. Thank God for what he gave you to work with.

You want balance. Show God that it is profitable to bless you. Why would God invest in you if he can't get a return from you? Give in proportion to how God has prospered you and break the curse of selfishness. Make sure nothing in your heart becomes an idol. Cast down every high thing, and keep yourself profitable. Pray that your hands remain open when God blesses you. It's better to humble yourself than have God do that.

You'll recognize your hidden idols when you can't give them up. What has God given you that you have the wrong attitude about? The prosperity formula is this: "Trust in the LORD and do good; dwell in the land and enjoy safe pasture" (Ps. 37:3 NIV). God is looking for someone to bless. "For the eyes of the LORD range throughout the earth to strengthen those whose hearts are fully committed to him" (2 Chron. 16:9 NIV). If your heart is right and you're ready to handle what's next, goodness and mercy will follow you.

Get rid of everything that's hindering the flow of God in your heart and environment. You'll have to break certain ties. Don't fool with stuff you can't handle—drive it out. Whenever God gives you something, get busy about possessing it. You can't make money in the heights if you perform in the shallows. Don't overinvest; don't allow others to get more out of you than they need. Don't worry about what people call fair. You have to allocate blessings according to ability, performance, faithfulness, and function. Give more to the more and less to the less. God is methodical, not impulsive. When you know something, straighten it out. Get fulfillment out of what God says.

PROMPT FOR REFLECTION

What desires has God put in your heart? What has he been empowering you to do regarding your finances?

PRAYER

Father, I thank you that I am under your unmerited favor. When you send blessings my way, I will see, appreciate, and enjoy them. I don't deserve any blessing from you, but you bless me nonetheless because you love me and because of what Jesus has done for me at the cross.

Father, I give you thanks, praise, and glory for all you have blessed me with and all you will bless me with. I thank you that you are aware of all things I need, and you want to add these things to me. Help me not worry about getting these things; help me make seeking Jesus and his righteousness my daily priority. I know that when I put you first in my life, everything else will fall into place for my good.

CHAPTER 7

Divine Family

> Whoever brings ruin on their family will inherit only
> wind, and the fool will be servant to the wise.
> —Proverbs 11:29 (NIV)

A close friend gave me insight about a lifestyle I did not know firsthand. My friend shared his testimony about how God had been at work in his life; he had joined a gang in his youth to stop being bullied in school. I was reminded how desperately people need others. He wanted to belong to a group that made him feel powerful and protected, something he'd felt deprived of. If he would have had a strong sense of family, love, and acceptance from other people, he would have never chosen that destructive lifestyle.

We have a natural hunger to be part of something that accepts, affirms, and appreciates us. The good news is that even if you have never received that from your biological family, God will set you up in a spiritual family, and that is just as important in many ways.

I was placed in a spiritual family, Bethel Church, while answering the call to grow in the Holy Spirit gifts, particularly the gift of prophecy. Through this family, I experienced what God had wanted for me. In this family, God is our Father and we are his kids. That meant I suddenly had a whole bunch of believers in Jesus who were my brothers and sisters. Being independent and introverted, I needed time to open up to them, but when I did, the quality of my life increased dramatically. I realized our relationships contributed to our success and it was important to be yoked with people who walked closely with God.

Accept that not everyone has the same heart you have even if others can convince you otherwise at times. Others' actions, not their words, indicate how they feel about you. What if your family members' behavior makes you uncomfortable? I prefer the biblical interpretation: "Above all else, guard your heart, for everything you do flows from it" (Prov. 4:23 NIV). This highlights how we all desperately need a place of belonging and a sense of family. It took me a while to realize this about myself because I hadn't always had it, and let's face it, you think you know people but then they surprise you.

If you find yourself craving these kinds of relationship, pray for godly friends to come into your life. In the meantime, here are some qualities to look for in your framily—friends who become like family.

- They tell you the truth in love. "Faithful are the wounds of a friend, but the kisses of an enemy are deceitful" (Prov. 27:6 KJV).
- They give you sound advice. "Ointment and perfume delight the heart, and the sweetness of a man's friend gives delight by hearty counsel" (Prov. 27:9 KJV).

- They refine you. "As iron sharpens iron, so a man sharpens the countenance of his friend" (Prov. 27:17 KJV).
- They help you grow in wisdom. "He who walks with wise men will be wise, but the companion of fools will be destroyed" (Prov. 13:20 KJV).
- They stay close to you. "A man who has friends must himself be friendly, but there is a friend who sticks closer than a brother" (Prov. 18:24 KJV).
- They love you and stand by you. "A friend loves at all times, and a brother is born for adversity" (Prov. 17:17 KJV).
- They help in a time of trouble. "Two are better than one, because they have a good reward for their labor. For if they fall, one will lift up his companion. But woe to him who is alone when he falls, for he has no one to help him up" (Eccl. 4:9–10 KJV).

If you are blessed with a family like this, protect your relationships with them by praying for and investing in them. If you desire more relationships like these, pray for that and for existing relationships that have less than desirable qualities. Pray. If you're not careful, you can pour out to people for years, minister to them, and touch their lives, but in one moment or by one mistake, they turn their backs on you.

Be discerning of the people in your life so you won't be fooled and think others have deeper wells than they actually do for you. Not everyone in your life is intended to be your family or friend, but you have to have at least a couple. In the book of Samuel, a strong friendship is clear: "Now it came about when he had finished speaking to Saul, that the soul of Jonathan was knit to the soul of David, and Jonathan loved him as himself"

(1 Samuel 18:1 NASB). Jonathan loved David as much as he loved his own soul. Jonathan was there for him and worked through the highs and lows with him. Are you believing God for friendships that help you reach your purpose? For people who will stick with you through the hard times?

We see another close relationship in the book of Ruth, where even a generational gap couldn't prevent a relationship from flourishing. "But Ruth replied, 'Don't urge me to leave you or turn back from you. Where you go I will go, and where you stay I will stay'" (Ruth 1:16–17 NIV). Ruth didn't care about the cost; she had found a relationship so valuable that she was willing to leave everything she knew to stay connect to her mother-in-law, Naomi. You should desire relationships like that; you should be like Ruth. How do you treat your family? What do those who see you at your best and worst say about you?

Family requires work. You don't realize how abnormal a thing is until you bring it to the light of God's Word. If you bring it only to the light of what's allowable in your family, heart, or soul, you'll always be right. When you measure a thing by God's Word, you may find out more about it. Have a family unit to work through not only pain but also to celebrate with. You were never meant to process or do life outside the context of a family.

You can't choose your biological family, but you can choose whom you walk with. You may not have known your need for these people. You may be still waiting for your tribe, or you may be surrounded by people you never imagined God would surround you with, but he has a plan for you to be rightly associated with others. While many broken homes have produced broken people who find it difficult to reestablish intimacy and trust in relationships, the right associations can bring years of healing.

The secret to success in any relationship is being willing to change. God has promised you a place, but you have to be intentional about examining what you need in your connections. God made a promise to those who belong to him: "To them I will give within my temple and its walls a memorial and a name better than sons and daughters; I will give them an everlasting name that will endure forever" (Isa. 56:5 NIV).

There is a place for you. If you don't feel you've found it, keep searching diligently for it. And don't be afraid to connect with godly people whose value you can discern, when what's in them changes what's in you, when their language affects you, and when you share convictions.

When you know your destiny has one God, you go with what he says regardless of whether you or other people like it. You don't have to be anyone else's reality; you can remain what God has called you to be. You can take your peace, sleep, rest, heart, and feelings out of others' hands.

Nobody is worth your communication with God. You need to be heard when you pray—the most important thing in your life. If something restricts your communication with God, everything you have can become a curse. You need to be able to talk to God and have him talk back.

God says that if you're coming to the altar but have an issue with anyone, go get reconciled to that person. He says that because if you are offended, you are not like him. The difference between Peter and Judas was that one was the devil from the beginning and the other was the devil for just a moment. Peter was the devil for a moment. At the end of his life, Jesus said he had lost none but the son of perdition who had been the devil from the beginning.

As a leader, friend, parent—whoever you are—discern your Peters and Judases. They will look the same; the difference is that one is having a moment but the other was that way from the start. They both made Jesus feel the same way. This is risky because you could miss out on developing a Peter because you're still mad at a Judas. You could be missing out on a redemptive opportunity because Judas taught you not to trust. But Judases and Peters are not the same. One is willing to learn from a mistake, to grow from a mistake, to say, "You're right, I'm sorry." The other will deny you and try to kill you. You have to decide on a case-by-case basis. This practice can to teach you to stop marking your brothers and sisters. Everybody is not the same. And every conflict is not the same. What's the same is you.

You need to do what love requires and not be scared to give or release—whatever it takes. Many of your family relationships would change if you started loving people beyond what they did; people are not what they do. If you get trapped and wrapped up in what people do, you'll begin to lose value for the person and become justified in your offense. But if you go before God, he will take over and answer the one who is clean. Be holy and have your heart clean; don't allow what someone did keep you out of alignment. The minute you start praying, God will check you and overlook an offense. You are either going to be right or reconciled. Either way, you run the risk of not being heard in heaven.

God wants you to be set up to be answered quickly. Come as you are, but come clean and repent before God. You must get your heart right. You could be the one who starts a chain reaction in your family. When you know you were born with God's spiritual DNA, you don't allow any other DNA operating in your life to compete. When you have spiritual DNA, you intentionally allow it to create a chain reaction in your life.

Just because you were born in the image of God and carry his DNA doesn't mean there was a chain reaction of that DNA taking place in your life. For some, church enhances their spiritual sides and starts that chain reaction that creates blessings and overflow. Others attend church to worship, or it's the one day of the week they dress up. Others attend church because they're still trying to drown out all the other DNA that's telling them they're not good enough and they'll never make it. They think God is pulling on them and don't know exactly what to make of it, but they know they want to start a chain reaction. It's not enough just to be touched, feel good about that, and go back living their lives. They're trying to create a chain reaction in the spirit realm. They are crazy enough to believe they can receive a word from God that will allow them to do supernatural things when they leave.

You have been called to create a chain reaction that generates love, kindness, purity, and faithfulness. The weapons of your warfare are not carnal. You can shake up generations. You can do something in your life that breaks down strongholds. It's not just about trying to live and find a rhythm; every time you turn on CNN or look at social media, you recognize that you are at war with something, and you can't just sit back and watch it happen. You start a ministry. You get refueled and recharged so you can go into the world and produce a chain reaction that serves notice on devils and demons that you are not someone to be messed with; you know whom your DNA is from.

Whether you were raised in a large or small family, you are surrounded by a great crowd of witnesses and you can change the spiritual DNA of your family. You may be the first one to take it this seriously, the first one to be connected the way you are, but your awakening can produce a chain reaction. If you track your spiritual DNA all the way back, you will stumble upon Jesus. When was the last time you recognized your spiritual DNA was not just about a message but about tracing your life back to the Son of God? You tap into that when you need change and supernatural strength. You're not in this life on your own; all you need to do is tap into your spiritual DNA, which raised Jesus from the grave and will raise you out of your circumstance and break depression off your life. You have spiritual DNA working on your behalf; heaven is backing you up. Start thinking about where in your family you need to start a chain reaction. What do you need to see reproduced and amplified? God can start a chain reaction of his DNA in your spirit that will change your patterns and rhythms. It can make bitterness flee and produce a spiritual reaction in your life.

If you keep your inner lamp burning, if you are crazy enough to walk by faith and believe that with God you can do the impossible, the generations after you will experience a chain reaction and win. You are the perfect one to demonstrate a godly marriage because you went through a divorce. You are the perfect one to demonstrate what it means to be a full and present parent because you have suffered through brokenness and addiction. You can break strongholds off your family because you know exactly what you're up against. You may be the only one who can do it. Give your heart a happy home for the sake of your family.

PROMPT FOR REFLECTION

Do you feel grounded in a spiritual or biological family? How is the quality of your relationships with your family?

PRAYER

Lord, I pray for my relationship with each of my family members. Specifically, I pray for my relationship with (name the family member for with whom you are most concerned). I pray you bring healing, reconciliation, and restoration where it is needed.

Bless our relationships, and make them strong. I pray for any relationship I have with people who don't know you, Lord. Give me words to say that will turn their hearts to you. Help me be your light for them. Specifically, I pray for (name an unbeliever or someone who has walked away from God). Soften this person's heat to open her (his) eyes to receive you and follow you faithfully. I pray for godly friends, role models, and mentors to come into my life. Send people who will speak the truth in love. Help me be strong in faith and raise the standards to which I aspire.

CHAPTER 8

Divine Relationships

Be completely humble and gentle; be patient, bearing one another in love. Make every effort to keep the unity of the Spirit through the bond of peace.
—Ephesians 4:2–3 NIV

So you want a relationship, but are you ready for it? Or maybe you're in one, so how do you change and improve it? What will help you position yourself for a good, godly relationship that deepens and matures into a God-ordained, God-anointed, and God-blessed one?

You need to know what the Word of God says about dating, courtship, and marriage. God has things to say about such matters, and it's impossible to love the ways the scripture instructs us without God's help.

The Lord made you to couple up; he gave you the desire to be in a relationship, and you may know you're destined to be in a kingdom partnership if you're not already, and you will be brought together to walk in purpose. But be ready and able to step into it by being obedient. "Trust in the Lord with all your heart and lean not on your own understanding; in all your ways submit to him, and he will make your paths straight" (Prov. 3:5–6 NIV).

Your way isn't God's way. He wants you to trust his and guard your heart especially when it comes to whom you choose to spend your life with. God knows what's best and who's best for you. He doesn't need your help; he needs your obedience.

Relationships are life, and cultivating the right connections can bring life or take from your life. In our fast-paced world, some have chosen to overlook their greatest assets while others have put in the time and hard work to learn, understand, and grow through forming and maintaining healthy relationships. Needing to be connected with a tribe or community is a very human thing, and if you pay attention, it is a very divine thing. Your vibe will attract your tribe, so it's vital that you understand all you can about who and what you're associating with so you can keep quality in your corner.

God created the human race for connection. God put a desire in the human heart for connection, which is why he walked with humans the way he did. Connection is a vital part of your development. Every major world agenda has connection at its core. People join around their convictions. They decide what and whom they'll belong to as a by-product of their convictions.

It takes diligent effort to connect right. You may have made many mistakes in attempting to be connected, or you may have struggled to understand different relationships. It won't be perfect particularly if you have been unconnected for a while. Connecting with others means running into their imperfections and experiencing things that test and may scare you. You'll have painful experiences, but if you don't allow them to keep you from connecting, you'll thrive. You have to be determined. If God gave you a context to associate with divine connections and belong, release yourself to find out how to connect. The Spirit of God will show you the way to be connected.

Your spirit of influence is nonnegotiable, scheduled, and needful, and it will happen. Many endure life challenges, threats, assaults, and attacks on their hearts; they are just people trying to obey God and their calling. If you don't have strong relationships to retreat to, your enemies invisible and physical will always get the best of you. Everybody was meant to have a place, but some people live their entire lives searching for their places. Some of them get tired and frustrated because they can't find one, and then they'll try to create a place for other people. After years of being abandoned, overlooked, and neglected, others become depressed. Not cultivating and nurturing the right connections can be devastating.

Often, the enemy can get us feeling hurt, offended, and brokenhearted. The offense mode is not a prosperous mode; we all have to check our hearts at times because we are not immune. People we thought would be our ride or die turn out not to be like that. At times, we have to do things to better ourselves so we don't get hung up. We must recognize our hurt and know everybody gets hurt and grieves over the brokenness and heartbreak because it's not in us to do to them what they did to us. We have to let go and let God handle it or we'll be thrown into a tailspin.

Deal with your issues before the offense begins working on you and you start coddling the pain of betrayal and hurt and are held back from everything God has for you. Your hurt will fester if you don't take care of it. The offense jumps on you and shows up through your language and how you handle people. Get back to your purpose, what God called you to do; let the main thing be the main thing. Stop letting people who have nothing to do with your destiny control your emotions.

Shut down life and evaluate your heart, which God uses to love people back to life. He's not fighting you because you're weak; he's fighting you because you're strong. Take care of yourself first.

You're attacked the most when you're about to ascend to another level and God is trying to see if he can trust you with it. You'll be in the same place if you don't delete people because you're afraid. Stop being mad, and don't let Satan use the little foxes to spoil the grapes. Focus on the thousands of people celebrating you. You're not bound, so go—birds of a feather flock together, and you have to go higher.

God closes the door because it's time for you to move and he doesn't want you to allow your heart to hurt anymore. If you are doing what he has called you to do, that's all that matters. Focus on this when you're preparing for and working out your relationships.

1. Accept. Take back ownership of your life; your destiny is never connected to anyone who walked out on you. That relationship is over, and there's no going back. You're free to move on.

2. Forgive. Forgive yourself and the person; let go and move on. Stop worrying about revenge or trying to teach somebody a lesson. Pray this: "God, I want to forgive, but I don't know how to get past who they are and what they've done to you, their character, and their lack of conscience." Thank God that he shut that door and continues to show you their character so you don't go back. He will heal you. Their character can't take you where you're going. Expose people who are distracting you.

Relationships are easy God's way: they either work or they don't. God doesn't want you in a relationship in which you're fighting all the time or taking people on as projects, and that includes friends. Learn how to take the strange seasons as a blessing; God is sifting and revealing character, so stop trying to stabilize what he's trying to keep you from. God moves things out of the way. There can be no termites eating your foundation while you're trying to build an empire. Communication kills assumption; speak your truth in love, let your heart be right, and let your yes be yes and no be no.

3. Learn. Learn what you did wrong and fix it. The college of life gets better, not bitter, and there are no student loans to pay back.

4. Create. Create a vivid new future; refuse to stay stuck in hate and anger. Be proof that God has healed you and that you are full of possibilities. See yourself happy, and allow yourself to cry and dream again.

5. Choose. Choose power instead of victimhood; move in silence, and keep your heart right.

6. Trust. God can't bless a mess, so trust his restitution; ask him to bring to your attention whatever is in you so you can deal with it.

Don't allow Satan to use people to keep you stuck; God will take care of that if you let him. Your job is to release and let God deal with it. When you're trying to protect yourself, you often end up blocking the very thing you desperately desire—connection. It's okay to be frustrated when you don't understand everything God is doing, but in those moments, you can really learn who God is. Allow confusion, questions, heartaches, and loneliness to push you deeper into God's presence.

Mistakes in life and relationships come from saying no to God. If you give God one yes, he can undo all your mistakes and launch you into what he destined you to do. What if you think you're walking with the person God has for you but you're not walking totally in obedience? If you don't see something right, it's likely you have a perverse or backward understanding of sex and its impact. You can't walk in your full strength unless you have an understanding and a revelation about sex and have that area of your life under control. You might think in terms of how certain things make you feel, but there is no reference in scripture to the benefits of sex being how it makes us feel because the purpose of sex isn't physical but spiritual.

Relationships need patience and preparation so that you have a foundation to build on. You can't fight with a weapon that hasn't been proven. You can't live with someone you don't know. You don't really know who someone is until you have a disagreement. Do you know whom you have? Do you know what they can do? Are you watching and listening? What skills are in your house? What needs to be developed?

Preparation means being willing to look like a fool for a while. Stop trying to impress everybody. Stop rushing into love. It's easy for someone to be exactly what you need for a couple of weeks or a month or so. Give yourself the chance to be courted, valued, and cherished before allowing someone to play with your feelings. If someone can't wait for you, you know where he or she stands—he or she doesn't think you're worth the sacrifice. Slow down; it's hard to know what's real if no one has put in the time.

You have to be prepared before you consider sex before marriage; you have to understand sex so you won't be bound up. When you understand you can't link your soul to just anybody, that will radically transform how you approach dating and courting. You will respect yourself enough that you will not intertwine your spirit with just anyone. Sex is not as simple as being casual, as just following what feels right; it is meant to create a soul tie, and what do you do when you have a soul tie to someone who is not your soulmate? You might not think about that and go with the flow, but what you don't think about has consequences you'll inevitably face.

If this is speaking to you, you can break free and give your sexuality back to Christ. A great book to reference is *The Wait*. Be informed, and surround yourself with support. As you desire God more and more, you will see other areas of your life that are competing with him. You don't want to conflict with God. When your desire for him becomes greater than your other desires, you will be able to pray for him to take it. You have to want him and hate what separate you from him.

When you pray sincerely for him to take it, the Holy Spirit will empower you. There is no spirit like the Holy Spirit, but you have to yield to God. Strength and deliverance in this area will allow you to be a testimony. Walk in freedom and clarity. When you give God your willingness to live a life of integrity before him, he will meet you.

Whatever is at the center of your life has the greatest pull on it and indicates what's going on in your heart and mind. Keep Jesus at the center especially in your relationships. Jesus was at the center of the manger scene, but what if he hadn't been? If relationships or Mary and Joseph are moved to the center, you suddenly begin focusing on the other person and start fixating on things you like or don't like. If you feel overlooked or mistreated, you can form an unhealthy pattern in your relationships because you are looking at the wrong person to establish your worth.

Only your Creator can establish your worth. If the wise men are moved to the center, or your own plans and logic are—and you decide what will happen and when—you'll likely become angry and frustrated when things don't go according to your plans and you can't dictate the timing.

Most of the time, God will have you walk through some measure of mystery, confusion, and silence regarding your future mate, and you have to learn to walk by faith and not take things into your own hands. God is constantly moving in ways you don't know, so when he seems silent, don't try to control things, don't get louder and move away, just get quieter and move closer to him.

What if the blanket and the lamb were at the center of the scene? They represent your comforts. How far do you usually get remaining in your comfort zone? God's plans require you to step away from your comforts and be willing to do something crazy, wild, and dangerous, something beyond your management and control.

We try to avoid turbulence; we want what is steady and smooth, but that's not why Jesus came to the world. We have time to criticize when we're not living our own adventures; we should get busy doing what God has called us to do. Comfort is the enemy of destiny; our steps will look different as God leads us into the relationships he has for us, so we shouldn't compare or settle; we should trust him.

Pursue the plan God has for your life and watch him unfold all the specifics as you move forward. When the Holy Spirit does this great unfolding in your life, you will see your purpose more clearly and great clarity will come. Embrace the season of unfolding; allow God to take you step by step. Don't rush the unfolding because God has the end in mind. Get prepared for what God has promised you.

The right connections and communities will help you realize things about yourself that you don't realize. Jesus sent his disciples two by two because he valued the power of connection. You won't know all your strengths and weaknesses without connections and communities. Without a team, you will live in and under your own perspective, which is flawed because it is not God's perspective. With the power you get from being connected, you will realize that what you think are your strengths may be weaknesses, that what you value may be worthless.

Whether it was through my athletic teams, school leadership projects, sorority engagements, work opportunities, hobbies, and many other experiences, God has blessed me to be connected with people. One of my greatest privileges is being able to walk with friends as they step into their dreams. There is nothing like being in a pure-hearted and like-minded community when you are vulnerable or when it's time for you to be celebrated. Divine associations truly bless your life in more ways than you can imagine or begin to ask for.

I've learned the hard way that mistakes often occur when we misjudge whom to trust with information and in some cases with our hearts. We thrive when we fill our hearts with those who pump the lifeblood of friendship, encouragement, and wise counsel into us. We must stand firm in faith. Anyone who leaves us can't stay, and anyone who stays can't leave.

God owns your life, but you care for it. Part of that is carefully deciding whom you team up with. Few of us make it on our own. To succeed, good leaders surround themselves with others who complement their strengths and weaknesses. Be picky about whom you keep around you. Personalities, words, and traits rub off naturally. Align with God and the right people. Get your intercessory team—you'll need them in battle.

Don't look at where you are; look at where you're going. Make sure you are connected to the right people in this season. Surround yourself with only those who will help you walk in the purposes and plans God has over your life. Paul wrote, "We do not want you to become lazy, but to imitate those who through faith and patience inherit what has been promised" (Heb. 6:12 NIV).

The hour we are in is a special time for the body of Christ; we must make sure the people around us are spiritually strong. We should grow close to those who have followed God all the way through their hard times. We must align ourselves with people who stay in the battle until they inherit the promises and the purposes God has for them.

Associations vary just as much as people do. Assess the state of your tribe. Whoever counted you out doesn't count. When you consider committing your time, energy, finances, professional endorsements, or any other contribution to a group, be willing to accept their liabilities as your own. You will be bound by their rules even if you disagree with them. You must not expect to receive something from your affiliations that they cannot provide you. Peel back the real motives of your heart or you will likely set yourself up for disappointment.

We all need relationships in which we know others have our back no matter what; they hold our arms up, they push us through to breakthroughs by praying and covering us. They are loyal and steadfast because they know they are where they were called to be.

People who are unhealthily attached to you are joy drainers. Keep a tribe of loyal and honest friends with you—no haters, backstabbers, or gossipers. Be the one who lifts others. Be the one others can trust. Have the courage to tell others when they have offended, hurt, or disappointed you. Drama doesn't just walk into your life out of nowhere, you either create it, invite it, or associate with people that bring it.

Pride works against real and authentic connections. Sometimes it's fear, but a lot of times it's pride, so no real connection works without humility, which is required in friendship. It takes humility to become a part of something bigger than yourself. Without it, you end up missing out on really seeing your value. You can't thoroughly see all that you are when you refuse to allow yourself to be accepted, to be celebrated, and to belong to something that's beyond what you realize or do.

You will learn more of your strengths through your connections than by self-discovery because you don't know what you don't know. Satan knows that as long as he keeps you alienated and isolated, you won't realize all your real strengths. Your real capacity will be discerned and will be triggered by your desires to be connected. If you're alone, it's easy to drift and become discouraged. If you drift too far, you risk becoming unhealthy and toxic.

Toxic people defy logic. Some are blissfully unaware of the negative impact they have on others, and others seem to derive satisfaction from creating chaos and pushing others' buttons. When considering those you choose to align with—and yes, it is a choice—learn how to deal with different kinds of people and know without a doubt that truly dysfunctional people will never be worth all the time and energy they will demand of you. These people shamelessly create unnecessary complexity, strife, and worst of all, stress. You really don't have time for that. Hans F. Hansen stated it simply: "People inspire you, or they drain you—pick them wisely."

To practically implement this wisdom, create and enforce your boundaries and deal breakers. Excellent people are skilled at controlling their emotions in times of stress. They can identify toxic people and keep them at bay. I once heard that we're the products of the five people we spend most of our time with. If you allow even one of those five to be toxic, you'll soon find how capable he or she is of holding you back.

Knowing who these people are gives you the ability to distance yourself from them. The trick is to separate those who simply annoy you from those who are truly toxic and need to be avoided and likely cut off. Here are some toxic tendencies to watch out for.

- arrogance/false confidence
- judgmental
- twisted
- vampires
- manipulators—master takers
- envious
- self-absorbed
- victims
- temperamental—no control over emotions
- gossips

People will drive you crazy if you let yourself be drawn into their facades and crazy-making. Their behavior is irrational, so it's no use trying to understand them and give them more time and attention; don't get sucked into their mess.

This is where the importance of co-laboring shows up. As we're walking with God and yielding to his direction, we'll receive wisdom to help us relate in godly ways. "Do not make friends with a hot-tempered person, do not associate with one easily angered, or you may learn their ways and get yourself ensnared" (Prov. 22:24 NIV).

People can be are angry, mean, bitter, and evil, and they can sow discord. Study Proverbs and use wisdom: "Walk with the wise and become wise. For a companion of fools suffers harm" (Prov. 13:20 NIV). You have been set free to live in freedom. Do not be drawn astray. Being prosperous isn't just about money and good health; invest in prosperous associations as well.

Some people ignore all the warning signs and then try to pray for God to save those who are keeping them in sin or confusion. Yes, you should pray for them but from a distance. Stop playing with fire. Worldly relationships will destroy you if you don't create boundaries and stop flirting with sin.

It would be great if you could just fast-forward time just to see where the relationship will lead, but you know better. Let God's Word be your mirror. Check yourself and be cleansed daily. In the presence of God, everything changes. Nothing is more powerful than your private daily time with the Lord.

We must have the presence of God flowing in and through us. "You make known to me the path of life; in Your presence there is fullness of joy; at your right hand are pleasures ever more" (Ps. 16:11 ESV). In this world, people have to know we are people of the presence. We can walk through trials, tests, and tribulations when we are stewards of God's presence. Remember that you're always one decision away from a totally different life.

After detoxing, reestablish your boundaries and deal breakers. Boundaries are the physical, emotional, and mental limits you establish to protect yourself from being manipulated, used, or violated by others. They allow you to separate who you are and what you think and feel from others' thoughts and feelings. Going a step further and filtering your boundaries through the Word of God allows you to base your foundation on truth rather than something easily changed.

Figure out your boundaries—what you're ready for and what you can and can't offer—before entering into any agreement or relationship if you want to function effectively. When you establish your boundaries, you are determining what you need in your relationships to feel safe and valued. It's about recognizing and honoring your feelings.

BOUNDARIES

Consider these types of boundaries.

- emotional—violated when someone criticizes, belittles, or invalidates your feelings
- physical—violated when others touch you in ways that make you feel uncomfortable or when they invade your personal space
- sexual—violated by unwanted sexual touch, pressure to engage in sexual acts, uninvited comments
- intellectual—violated when someone dismisses or belittles your thoughts or ideas
- time—violated when another demands too much of your time, isolates you, or doesn't show up when promised
- material—violated when others take or damage your things or when they pressure you to give or lend them your possessions or money
- spiritual—violated when someone uses religion to control or belittle your beliefs

You never have to tolerate boundary violations. Those who have problems with your boundaries aren't good candidates for any relationship. You must enforce your boundaries for them to be effective. People who are manipulators purposely violate your boundaries to see what you will tolerate.

DEAL BREAKERS

Deal breakers are those things you won't compromise, things you'll never tolerate. Some examples of deal breakers are lying, infidelity, unwillingness to engage in healthy communication, blaming, avoiding, and manipulating.

These protect your emotional security and stability. You don't need to communicate this up-front like boundaries, but if others violate one, you need to thank them for the good times, walk away, and mean it.

People can put on a good show especially if you reveal too much information too quickly. Actions are louder than words. Don't turn any red flags white to keep the peace and avoid confrontation. Respect yourself and keep your integrity intact.

Here are a few check and balances of who can't go with you.

1. They're drama. There is always something and it's never anything positive or building; it's something that is heavy and brings confusion to your otherwise peaceful and contented state. Some of you know when you shouldn't answer the phone but you answer it anyway. Anyone who is not a peacemaker and is not calling to encourage you but to drop a mess on you cannot be your friend.

2. They don't pray and encourage you. Iron sharpens iron, so if you have someone in your life who would rather give advice and gossip but will not pray and encourage

you, ask yourself if that person is really sharpening you or if you're allowing yourself to become dull.

3. They're competitive. A spirit of competition is not welcome where you are going. Someone who is always making withdrawals, never deposits, or someone who is always trying to outdo you is not looking after your righteousness and well-being.

    Secret jealousy is a frenemy. Your friends do not compete with you; they stay in their lanes and do what God is calling them to do. They will encourage and challenge you, but they will not try to copy your vision or diminish your dream and anointing. Copycat spirits will never win against anointed spirits. Their rejection is God's protection. The enemy wants to steal your peace and joy and can work through people. Don't accept fake friends. What God has for you is for you.

4. They're friends in private but not in public. Those who can't be public about their support for us are not being led by the Holy Spirit. He knows how to move us to genuinely support people, and it's never about us.

    We need people who support us even if it's not about them, and we need to do the same thing. We should let the Spirit lead us, not others' approval or recognition. Friendships are not one-sided. Many of the hurts we experience come from our connecting with one-sided people. We show up for them and are willing to adjust what we have going on to be there for them, but when we have something important, where are they?

    Anyone who doesn't have good intentions but wants to zap into your life cannot be part of your life. Friends do not come to kill, steal, or destroy—the devil does. Surround yourself with people who can celebrate you. Pull back and you'll see who your friends are.

5. They're always bringing up your past. God is not a God of the past. Those who are constantly bringing up your past won't be able to see and encourage your future and will not push you to a level up. Being pulled into your past will steal your present. Those who can't stand your now either from jealousy or intimidation will not build you up and keep you encouraged. They will not bring you life if they want to live in dead things.

    If the season has changed and they cannot walk the journey of wholeness and evolve with you, they are likely not beneficial to your growth and what God is doing now. They will make you feel heavy and burdened. Don't let anyone become dead weight. Guard what God has for you, your personal space, and your anointing.

Your friends are those whom you know and with whom you have mutual affection. Those who bring up your past don't know you now. The affection in friendship has to be mutual. When you are getting to know someone, make sure he or she is your friend first. You need real people of God and real and relevant words in your life. "Do not be misled, bad company corrupts good character" (1 Cor. 15:33 NIV). Do not be misled by confusion and allow your spirit to be run down. Proverbs says, "One who has unreliable friends soon comes to ruin" (Prov. 18:24 NIV). People you cannot depend on are unreliable; the Word of God backs that up. If you hang around unreliable friends, they will bring you down and destroy everything you've worked for, so be careful about that.

Here's the good news; you have a friend who sticks closer than a brother does—Jesus. Make him your best friend. You can go to and pray to him and trust that what you said to him in private will not be spread all over the world. What a friend you have in Jesus. What a privilege it is to take everything to God in prayer. Stop the spirit of rejection in its tracks. When you make Jesus your best friend, he will be the author and finisher of your faith. He knows what you need and whom you need. He will place the right people in your life. Makes Jesus your all and all, and let him guide you to and through your relationships.

PROMPT FOR REFLECTION

Are you ready for the relationship God has for you? Have you healed from past hurts? Is God still at the center, or has a relationship become an idol?

PRAYER

Lord, I come humbly before you and ask you to cleanse my heart of every fault and renew a right spirit in me. Forgive me for thoughts I have had, words I have spoken, and things I have done that do not glorify you or contradict your commands. Specifically, I confess to you (name any thoughts, words or actions that you know are not pleasing to God). I confess it as sin, and I repent of it. I choose to walk away from my unhealthy relationships. I commit to trusting you with my whole being. I declare you to be Lord over every area of my life today and every day.

CHAPTER 9

Divine Health

> Do not be wise in your own eyes; fear the Lord
> and shun evil. This will bring health to your
> body and nourishment to your bones.
> —Proverbs 3:7–8 NIV

> Blessed is the one who does not walk in step with the wicked or stand in the way the sinners take or sit in the company of mockers, but whose delight is in the law of the Lord, and who meditates on his law day and night. That person is like a tree planted by streams of water, which yields fruit in season and whose leaf does not wither-whatever they do prospers. (Ps. 1:1–3 NIV)

Does this sound like you? Do you want it to? What in your history makes intimacy with God difficult?

This verse tells us we often have been out of alignment so long that misalignment feels normal. Consider going to a chiropractor. Initially, there is some sort of pain that leads you to go to the appointment. Once you get aligned, the chiropractor starts finding several other things out of alignment that you've learned to live with.

Often when it comes to health, it isn't until this area gets what you considered really bad that you make the decision to manage the issues because you've learned how to function out of alignment. So what is alignment? "Before I formed you in the womb, I knew you, before you were born, I set you apart" (Jer. 1:5 NIV). Before you even got your start on this earth, God knew you, what you were supposed to look like, who you were supposed to be connected to, who you were not supposed to be connected to, where you were supposed to live, and how you were supposed to think and function.

God has already seen you. Jeremiah reassured you that God knew the plans he had for you—plans to prosper you, not harm you—to give you a future and a hope. He's already seen you and has plans to move you toward what he saw.

Alignment is about his getting you to a place where you can grow and move without hindrance. What's *not* happening is one of the most powerful forces working for you. The nots, the knots, can stifle your destiny, so you have to figure out what they are and get them out so you can flourish. Masseuses get your knots out and align you; God gets your nots out and aligns you; in both cases, they get your body flowing the way it was meant to flow and thrive.

The biblical David had a lot of knots in his life, but he learned to work them out. During the alignment process, things move and shift, and that can be uncomfortable. Misalignment can feel more comfortable than being aligned because we're so used to being in misalignment. Getting aligned is painful and costly. Until you accept that God has to get some nots out of you, you'll find yourself weeping over what's not ordained for your life.

Let your delight be in the law of the Lord. When you discover what the word is over your life and when you align with it, you will flow in something that cannot be hindered, and that's alignment. Likely, God has done things in your life but you haven't come to terms with the fact that they were blessings. Sometimes, God is so good that he'll allow you to release the longing for things you don't want to give up, and you stop chasing after them. You don't like how it took place, but you know God is killing your desire for what is out of alignment and replacing it with what he wants.

It may take a while to get to where you feel whatever you are doing is prospering, but God at least has shown you what healthy alignment is—a tree that brings forth fruit in its season. There are times to grow, become, and then produce. Just because you don't see fruit doesn't mean you're not aligned. You won't see fruit in a season when it's not meant to be. If you stay planted by the river, you'll come into your season. You've tapped into a river that will never run dry, and when you season comes, you will bear fruit.

When your inner self is aligned, your outer self will follow. People count you out when they don't see fruit, but what they don't know is when you're not growing on the outside, you're growing on the inside. You can force things if you want to, but that will not bring you into alignment and may create a bigger mess for you. Don't think because getting into alignment hurts or you don't see fruit that you're out of alignment.

When you are aligned, you can become the healthiest version of you. The future is catching up with what God knew. You've sown seeds, your heart is pure, you fought your Goliaths, and you haven't allowed stress to strip your identity—it's your time. The alignment has been happening on the inside, and you will see it and give God the glory.

Alignment also exposes what's hiding in your blind spots, and that can be scary. Inner giants are relentless, but be committed to becoming your best and getting the wrong things out of the way. Sometimes, the right thing coming into your life will reveal everything that's wrong with you. If you aren't careful, you'll run from the challenge God designed to manifest who you are and his calling on you. When you're in alignment, you will attract the right things to you, but that doesn't mean they will come easily.

It's time to become. God will reposition you, and you'll have to be cool with letting it happen. Come to terms that it was God and move on. God has better in front of you. It's not about how it happened; it's about God getting you to where you need to be. New things will challenge you because you've been more comfortable in misalignment, but don't squander them. They will challenge you to become something you've never been—a stranger to you but not to God. Let him bring clarity to you. Close the wrong doors so you can run boldly through the open one. Trust in him and what he is doing. In Genesis, Jacob wrestled with alignment until he caught up with his name Israel.

The support you need above all physical healing is divine assistance to see and savor God's glory. This is the only way to keep the faith and persevere to the end. As you behold the glory of God in his Word, you are being renewed and transformed; you are coming into alignment with divine healing. By setting your mind on things above, you are feeding your soul the truth and putting all other wrong appetites to death.

Jesus invites us to a different lifestyle. He calls us to the small, everyday things—prayer, silence, solitude, Sabbath—because in doing them, we find the rest he speaks of. These practices will help you to draw closer to Jesus, your healthiest position.

1. Pray. Your soul hungers and thirsts for God. It needs to walk and talk with your Creator. Prayer is simply talking to God. He asks you to come as you are, and he reveals his glory to you. You can pray driving to and from work, before and after meetings, during quiet time, or while washing dishes. Just pray without ceasing.

2. Confess. If you've committed to walk in the light, you've admitted that you were walking in darkness. Recognize your brokenness and confess it to your Savior. Confessing and turning away from sin that prevents you from walking openly with God will make you feel lighter, grateful that you don't have to carry that weight, and thankful that your Creator loves you and wants you to experience freedom. Confession also helps you cultivate and open and honest relationship with God.

3. Meditate. Meditation will help you empty yourself of the noise and distractions of the world and fill yourself with the person and the Word of God. This is unlike the Eastern concept of meditation, which aims mostly at emptying oneself to achieve oneness with the universe. Instead, meditation makes you more fully alive, complete, and truly you as you contemplate God and his attributes. It's a divine encounter in which you become in sync with Christ's mind.

4. Study. Yes, study. This is more than contemplation. Your soul longs to know God and be known by him perfectly in return. The Holy Spirit animates the Word and helps you receive and apply its timely and personal messages. It also judges your thoughts and attitudes.

When you have a greater appetite for God's Word, he will give you greater knowledge of himself.

5. Fast. Fasting is not for dieting or for show but to draw closer to God and better understand your deep need for him. Often, what you are hungry for is God, and fasting reminds you of that. As you fast, you begin to see that you are not hungry for food, others' approval, or anything other than a deeper connection with God. It reminds you that God abundantly provides for all your needs.

6. Respect the Sabbath. Resting from your labors is a declaration that God alone sustains you, that you're not the one who keeps the world running. When you stop striving for one day a week, you interact with God the way he intended. If you find yourself reaching burnout, that means your soul is crying for rest.

7. Give. Giving goes way beyond giving your money; it includes giving your time, talents, and resources. Giving reminds you that life isn't about being self-absorbed or materialistic and that your deepest enjoyment comes from God's presence.

As you give and serve, you remember your value does not come from the need to prove your greatness but in your relationship with God. You begin to really know God's heart as you give.

A few months before a very emotionally challenging season, I was led to begin a no-sugar diet, something I had never done before and was not enthused about. I loved sugar and carbs, but God knew I'd need to be healthier to handle what I was about to walk through. Like anything else, I resisted it in the beginning. I didn't know what new appliances I'd need, what my new grocery list would look like, or how I'd manage adding new meals to cook to my schedule. But one step at a time, I adjusted and found a new rhythm that I maintain today.

Do I recommend removing sugar from your diet? Yes, but not necessarily. What's best is asking God to lead you in the ways he wants to help you experience the full benefits of divine health.

You can control the direction your health is heading; you just need a clear path to do that. Health in its most basic form comes down to habits. You have to want to be better. Let your yielding to God be your measure of success; if you stop growing, you start dying inside. Do something every day that commits you to fulfillment and makes you follow through. It's structure; if you don't develop the rituals, you're killing yourself. When everything is in alignment and nothing is pulling you away, you'll progress.

Real health is keeping your faith up while sickness is wearing masks. Let God heal you; he knows who you are. God knows you'll go through things that feel like setbacks, but they are meant to prepare you for the seasons when he'll use you more than you imagined. Stop going through the motions; release things to God and build your faith back up.

There isn't anything in this world like living a transparent life before the Father. Trying to mask the ugliness of pain is work. Appearing holy in everyone's eyes is not worth it if your character is ugly. Know that you're not perfect and you need Jesus as we all do. Being obedient to God will take you to another level and be delivered. When your heart's posture changes, you'll become so free and will be put back together; your joy will flow naturally.

You talk yourself out of your spiritual life by refusing to be real about who and where you are. Until you start living right, you are not useful. Come home to God and let him do the heavy lifting. Once you admit how unloving and lost you are, Jesus will show up unexpectedly. You do not have all the answers, God does, and he will never leave or forsake you. He will push you to break through and not break down, and he never slips your secrets. You aren't like anyone else, so don't worry about what you're supposed to look like, and don't fall for the mask scheme. Let go, and don't pick up the bondage again; decide and commit. You are not stuck unless you want to be. Think bigger; old things have passed away, so dare to walk in the new. That's revival and true health.

PROMPT FOR REFLECTION

How do you define health? What does the Word of God say health is?

PRAYER

Lord, I come humbly before you and ask you to cleanse my spirit of every fault and renew a right spirit in me. Forgive me for thoughts I have had, words I have spoken, and things I have done that do not glorify you or contradict your commands. Specifically, I confess to you (name any thoughts, words, or actions that you know are not pleasing to God). I confess it as sin and repent of it. I choose to walk away from this pattern of thought or action and live your way. I know you are gracious and merciful, slow to anger, and of great kindness. Forgive me for ever taking that for granted.

CHAPTER 10

Divine Growth

For this reason, also, since the day we heard of it, we have not ceased to pray for you and to ask that you may be filled with the knowledge of His will in all spiritual wisdom and understanding, so that you will walk in a manner worthy of the Lord, to please Him in all respects, bearing fruit in every good work and increasing in the knowledge of God.
—Colossians 1:9–10 (NIV)

When you start exploring what God's power can do in your life, you will find how keeping your hope in him can maintain your peace of mind. As you continue walking with God, take some daily actions to ensure you are turning your will over to him.

We ask God to perform miracles that could have been unnecessary if we took care of life regularly. It doesn't matter how long we've been walking with God; we need to constantly search our hearts to make sure they are pure before God and we are wholly surrendered to him and what he wants to do in and through us. "Be diligent in these matters; give yourself wholly to them, so that everyone may see your progress" (1 Tim. 4:15 NIV).

How did David go back into life after he slew Goliath? It had to have been surprising for him to tap into a potential he hadn't necessarily tapped into until then. You need to tap into potential you didn't know you had before; if you speak prophetically what you believe by faith but don't see, you'll start seeing spiritually how God sees you.

In Samuel, David was beginning to gain King Saul's attention.

> Now it had happened as they were coming home, when David was returning from the slaughter of the Philistine, that the women had come out of all the cities of Israel, singing and dancing, to meet King Saul, with tambourines, with joy, and with musical instruments. So the women sang as they danced, and said: "Saul has slain his thousands, And David his ten thousands." (1 Sam. 18:6–7 NKJV)

You know there's something unique about you, but you haven't found your lane yet. Others recognize something special about you too but haven't quite found what box to put you in. If you aren't careful, you might let the fact that someone has a crown make you believe you don't have one. Don't be alarmed when it looks as if someone is in your spot; you've tapped into your royalty but haven't found your crown yet.

When God decides to do a new thing, the old thing isn't safe anymore. When you wrestle with believing God, you don't burn your bridges, and doubt begins to pull a number on you. Sometimes, faith is for your deliverance because doubt will have you thinking and creating scenarios that disorient you.

In a moment when they should have been celebrating promises of their future, the Israelites had evidence in front of them; they should have been rejoicing about their destiny that was on the way, but instead, they cried even though it wasn't a sad time but a happy time. When you don't believe the promises of God, you leave yourself open to deception and disorientation. If the wrong thing is in position, the right thing can't get to you. God will sometimes remove the wrong thing to get you to the right thing. You can help him by burning your bridges.

Crying in a season where you should be rejoicing is plain wrong; it's a reminder of how easy it is to look back. You gravitate toward the past because it was reality and the present and future are unknown; you like the comfort and convenience of what you know so much that you'd even sacrifice what could be by clinging to what was. Break the fear of the unknown; you may not know it, but God does. Where you are going is irrelevant; the only thing that matters is who is ordering your steps. If God is, you're going somewhere higher. Claim in confidence that God is ordering your steps.

Understand what God expects of you when he gives you a word, which will be prophetic. He expects this word to become your new reality. God doesn't waste a single word; he is that word. When he gives you the word, he is giving you a piece of himself and expecting you to take him at his word, not doubt it. That is your only responsibility. Will you believe or question his word that has hit you in your spirit? God knows how to validate his word to you; he gave you an ear to hear and a spirit to discern when he speaks. His sheep know him, so you are left without excuse.

God expects your reality to shift when he speaks to you. In that particular area, you will no longer live by what you see but by what God said. Your new reality is based on what he said, but when you don't live in that reality, the wilderness grows. The moment you decide to believe God, it will be so. Are you in the wilderness because you haven't believed?

You have to keep a Promised Land mentality to endure the wilderness. Sometimes, seasons have nothing to do with your faith and everything to do with your development. God shows you things in the wilderness that you could never see in the Promised Land. You will endure some wilderness seasons and learn to balance circumstances with his promises because you know he has a plan for your life.

Jesus didn't look at what he had to go through; he looked at what he had to get to. You have to hear and receive the promise to have this mentality. There is a correlating promise for every season of your life. If you are properly motivated by the promise, you won't be intimidated by the process.

Thankfully for the Israelites, Joshua and Caleb encouraged the children of Israel who were talking crazy. No leader strokes and confirms mediocrity. If the giants in your way seem intimidated, it means you're not seeing the promise right. Your fear is evidence that you have disconnected from the promise, so if you feel fear and intimidation somewhere in the promise, you've lost sight of what is ahead. Knowing it is true will give you courage in the face of whatever you must go through. Joshua and Caleb said,

> The land we passed through and explored is exceedingly good. If the LORD is pleased with us, he will lead us into that land, a land flowing with milk and honey, and will give it to us. Only do not rebel against the LORD. And do not be afraid of the people of the land, because we

will devour them. Their protection is gone, but the LORD is with us. Do not be afraid of them. (Num. 14:7–9 NIV)

They were reassuring them of the promise, not talking about the giants. They were getting them excited about what was next. If they were in alignment with the Lord's leadership, it was a done deal. Seeing the promise correctly helps you see the giant correctly. If you're in alignment and God spoke it, no one will be able to stand before you.

Your giants lose their power when God's hand is on your life. If God is for you, who can be against you? God will take away their power and grant you victory. What you're calling a battle is really bread. Heaven is backing you up right now.

In the case of Ruth, who suddenly lost her husband and the life she knew, we learn that sometimes in the wilderness, one of the hardest things to get over is yourself. Every time you go through something, you lose something. You're not quite the same. You're a survivor because you came through it, but sometimes, surviving it doesn't feel as good as you thought it would. You've survived, but you're too tired to celebrate that. You're reaching out for something but don't know how much it'll cost you.

After losing her husband, Ruth refused to let her mother-in-law Naomi leave her: "Don't urge me to leave you or turn back from you. Where you go, I will go, and where you stay I will stay. Your people will be my people and your God my God" (Ruth 1:16–17 NLT).

The name Naomi means joy. You may not have joy; you did when you started out, but life will take the gleam out of your eye. Ruth is the story of an empty woman coming to a full place; the famine was over, but you think a famine is starting in you. You know that to gather anything, you have to have some joy, but you convince yourself that you have nothing left to give. You've given everything you had—every ounce of courage. Your life as you imagined it is over.

At some point, you have to say goodbye to things, and the hardest goodbyes in the world are the goodbyes to things you had in mind, things you thought you needed, things that were a part of your life, and you don't have anything else to give anymore; you've reached that point. Your life as you had imagined it has slipped away. You never thought it would cost so much to survive, to make it, to keep on keeping on.

The worst part isn't what you had to let go but what you had to kiss goodbye—a habit, an attitude, a way you saw yourself. They served a purpose at one time, but you've outgrown them; they've gone as far as they can go with you. You can't imagine what the future holds, but the Holy Spirit will make you give up everything you can see for everything you can't. Thank God for all that left and all that stayed, and then go on.

Sometimes, God asks you to stop pursuing your desires just to prove you can focus solely on Jesus. If you can't stay with Jesus as you grow, how likely are you to remain faithful at the harvest? Sometimes, your longing for something can make it practically an idol, and that could shift your position to unanswered prayer status. When that happens, the Lord will often instruct you to stop looking and pursue things outside yourself. Sometimes, he will give you a dream so large and unlikely that you have no choice but to depend completely on him. He does so to ensure he alone will get the glory; he has already appointed the time to release it to you, but first, he needs to test your obedience and faith. Seek ye first his kingdom! Always give God your best. He is a good God and deserves it. Doubt increases with inaction, but clarity reveals itself in momentum. Growth comes from progress. For all these reasons, keep going.

Expectation is the state of thinking or hoping that something, especially something pleasant, will happen. Some synonyms are anticipation, eagerness, excitement, and outlook. Expectation says no matter how long it takes, God will keep his promise.

In 2 Chronicles is a call to change our battle plan forever. Jehoshaphat started his prayer by acknowledging how great, awesome, powerful, and wonderful the Lord was and related specific mighty acts the Lord had performed to protect his people and uphold the promises he had made to them. Then he finally presented his request and expressed his confidence that God would handle the problem.

When you ask God for help, remember that he hears you the first time; you don't need to ask him over and over. You may do that just to reassure yourself that a breakthrough is coming, but you don't have to do that to move God. He has a plan for your deliverance from every situation even before one presents itself. He knows what you need before you ask him. God is not surprised when the enemy attacks. Your job is to focus on him and his mighty power, worship him, praise him for his solution, and listen for his direction. God always has the winning battle plan.

> You will not have to fight this battle. Take up your positions; stand firm and see the deliverance the LORD will give you, Judah and Jerusalem. Do not be afraid; do not be discouraged. Go out to face them tomorrow, and the LORD will be with you. (2 Chron. 20:17 NIV)

Abide in the Lord continually by focusing on him and doing what he directs you to do; guard against moving in your own flesh. There is no such thing as the rest of God without opposition. His rest is a spiritual rest, and it operates during storms. Jesus gave you an approach to the storm, not the promise of stagnation. Believe in the Lord your God and you shall be established; believe and remain steadfast and you shall prosper. Realize you have no might against your enemies by yourself. Recognize you don't know what to do. Submit to keeping your eyes on God.

As you seek God, he will show you your part in the battles you face. You can do it only in his strength and wisdom; the battle is his to win. God gives words of encouragement and instruction. You are to wait on him until he has told you what to do, and then you are to do it in the strength he gave you while you waited on him. And add a little extra praise because praise confuses the enemy. Lift your eyes and look at all the possibilities, not the problems you see; trust God to lead you to an even better situation. Live in the hope and joy that God promises to see you through to abundance and victory.

Deciding to trust God rather than stressing out will fix your problems. Regardless of the outcome, trust God. Some things may not turn out as you expected, but that's okay. Your hope is in the Lord, not a temporary situation. God works things out for your good as you live for him. If you're breathing at all, praise him. Don't be discouraged. God has more for you. He's refining you and making you an image-bearing son or daughter of heaven. He allows you to feel the tension between who you are and who he has created you to be as he moves you into the fullness of his hope and promise for your life. Don't run from the tension—lean into it.

You may have an awareness of your God-given potential, but at times, it can seem inactive in your life. God is calling you to travel further up and further in, to enter new dimensions of his freedom, love, grace, and power. Know that you are standing on the threshold of great promise. God squeezes you like a sponge so you can see what comes out.

Discipline is discipleship so that you can partake of his holiness without which you cannot know him. He chastens those he loves. He wants to remove the wrong things in you so you will be free of their weight and experience more of his glory and power.

If God were to squeeze you, what would come out? Would that rid yourself of anything not of him? Would you find yourself fully alive and experiencing God's greatest and best for your life? Be smarter than to be the only thing standing in your way. It's time to be bold about who you really are.

You were made to reflect the worth of your maker by being more satisfied in God than you are in anything else, and you know that. You magnify the worth of what you enjoy most. Without the Holy Spirit's new birth, you cannot enjoy God the way he deserves. God expects you to glorify him. The Bible says to do everything you do for God's glory. You were made to find God as well as happiness, joy, and satisfaction; these things are not at odds. Are you willing to lay down your life and desires and choose God's will for you? "Then he called the crowd to him along with his disciples and said: 'Whoever wants to be my disciple must deny themselves and take up their cross and follow me'" (Mark 8:34 NIV). The question is what puts these at odds. God never intended for these to be alternatives you choose. God is glorified in your being happy in him.

The pursuit of God's glory is the ultimate growth goal. God does everything to uphold and communicate his glory to you. Get God in you glorifying God; that's the Holy Spirit at work in you. You will know where you line up, whether you're at home with this—your willingness to throw God away. Your longing, wanting, aching, and yearning is found in delighting in the Lord. The mandate from God to enjoy God is central. It's not a willpower religion of doing things you don't want to do. If you don't want God more than you want anything, you haven't experienced the new birth. It puts the parts of you that are in love with the world in love with God. Your heart has to be changed if you want to be a believer; you need new passions, longings, and desires. Everything else is lesser than the surpassing greatness of knowing your Savior.

God is most glorified in us when we are most satisfied in him. God is glorified in his glory being seen and rejoiced in. The apostle Paul's deepest desire was to die to himself so he could live in Christ. As we die, we lose everything on earth but gain so much more—Jesus. Christ was most magnified in Paul's dying because in his dying, he was in Christ.

The quest for truth and the quest for joy are one. The way to know for sure what is true and how to find our supreme pleasure is by seeing the glory of God in his Word; we can experience scripture's power and truths and the self-authenticating glory of God; whoever has eyes to see will know this is God's Word. When the veil is lifted, we will see the glory of God in his Word; the eyes of our understanding will be enlightened, and we will be certain of it and satisfied by it.

The light of the gospel becomes real when you understand that the glory, the energy of Christ, is the heart of the good news. God shines light on darkness to give you knowledge of his glory; this is your new birth. You are undeniably a true and alive treasure. When you are born again, God grants you certainty and satisfaction. He opens your eyes to his glory in his Word, which is real and rewarding. In the light of glory, you know for sure and rejoice forever: "Let your light so shine before men, that they may see your good works and glorify your Father in heaven" (Matt. 5:16 NKJV).

God is glorious; if we trust his promises, we will make him look glorious.

> The Son is the radiance of God's glory and the exact representation of his being, sustaining all things by his powerful word. After he had provided purification for sins, he sat down at the right hand of the Majesty in heaven. (Heb. 1:3 NIV)

God is spirit surrounded by light, and everything bows in recognition of him. Don't be so busy looking at sin that you don't tap into God's glory.

Grit is going from glory to glory; it's when you put yourself in the position where you need grace again. Live a life that requires more grace. Satan will work relentlessly to make you wonder if you really have good seed. He tries to sow doubt, issues, fears, and insecurities in so you can't find your seed. But if you can find you enemy, you can find your seed because he always goes after what gives life. Your seed is where you feel the most doubt and insecurity. If you'll just let God keep doing the work in you, you'll have the grit to know there is tare in the field, but it will be so much easier at harvest time.

Do you have the grit, consciousness, flexibility, and vulnerability to grow to the next level of glory? Do you have the grit to receive what you are praying for? If you don't have grit, you'll end up frustrated. Recognize the power you have to let God's grace radically transform your life. Do you have the character to reap the harvest that comes with good seed? Ask God to tell you whom you need to become to produce what's already in you. Ask him to give you wisdom to see not just what didn't work out but also what you have produced. It's time to resurrect your grit.

PROMPT FOR REFLECTION

Where is God prompting you to grow? Are you expecting God to show up? Are you ready for your next opportunity?

PRAYER

In those places where I feel like sighing, may Jesus put a new song in my heart. Where I'm weary from holding on, may he give me new courage to stand strong. Where I've waited long to see the breakthrough, may he very soon do what only he can do. Sometimes, it feels that he's slow to intervene, but the truth is that he's meticulous and miraculous, sovereign and strategic. He knows what he's doing, and he deserves my trust.

Chapter 11

Divine Elevation

Every good and perfect gift is from above, coming down from the Father of the heavenly lights, who does not change like shifting shadows.
—James 1:17 NIV

Every good thing, every perfect gift comes from above. God's grace is available to anyone who wants some. The apostle Paul taught James of this grace. James said that gifts were given, but what's fascinating is that James, a works guy, believed we had to suffer and work for whatever we're given. Can you relate? James told us we were gifted, but many can't see others' gifts because they can't see their own. When it comes to elevation, we have to know what we've received.

Maybe you've been raised in an environment in which you can celebrate others' gifts but you've never recognized your own. This may come as a fresh word then—everything God created is gifted. You've been taught to be so humble that you are in denial about the fact that you are gifted. Because Satan is fighting you over your gift, you might at least acknowledge it. You paid for it, cried for it, lied over it, hated over it, and sweated over it. Isn't it about time you celebrated yourself? Whoever meets you gets something; when you walk into a room, you're an asset to everyone there. Satan wouldn't have been trying to fight you, discourage you, and break you down if you didn't have something.

You don't have to be famous to be gifted. Just because your gift doesn't put you on a stage doesn't mean you're not valuable. This is your time not to be intimidated but to walk in confidence and do something with your gift. You might as well say thank you to all your enemies because they taught you when they fought you that you were gifted. Learn how to appreciate the people who attacked you and realize how valuable you are for yourself. You've been beaten down long enough that it's time to receive the truth about who you are.

There will never ever be another you anytime or anywhere. You're in a class by yourself. Everything about you is unique; you're a designer original. Your gift didn't come to you by accident; God blessed you to do what you do.

Your gift will make room for you; stand by the doors in your life and your gift will open them and make ways where there seems to be none. Don't compromise your principles, don't take back your word, and don't hang your head. Praise God that he thought enough of you to design you for such times. Celebrate and appreciate what he's endowed you with. Satan doesn't want you to know what you have, but the devil is a liar. Praise God; you are the King's child; the Father of light designed you.

James called him the generator and producer of light. Darkness is the lack of light in a room; when light walks in, darkness walks out. When you are light, you affect everything around you and darkness has no reality. All you have to do is be there and darkness flees.

Elevation is God getting ready to shine a light on your gift so you'll know what you have and can use it. Don't walk away from what needs your attention. If you're not really there, you can't grow and what you've been called to change won't change. Nothing grows where there is no light. Get down into areas where you need to have dominion. You need to be running it, not running from it. God has not changed. You still have every gift and calling you have. God knows your weaknesses and sins but hasn't changed his mind about you. Just because there was variableness in you doesn't mean there's variableness in him; he changes not. Come to your senses. He has blessings he's ready to release on your behalf. All you must do is show up.

The darkness is not real. Repent for running, hiding, being distracted, complaining about things that don't matter, and chasing down the wrong things. Thank him for giving you another chance. Rebuke the darkness. Don't be where the enemy expects you to be; get out of your normal—break out and take flight. It's time to rise and shine because your light has come. When the glory of God enters your life, it will bring great breakthroughs, great miracles, and great blessings. God does not want you to live your life small; he wants you to have influence. Only Satan tries to limit you and make you small.

Elevation isn't about God doing what you want; it's about you doing what God wants you to do. He shouldn't have to force you to do anything. If you do not seek him first and honor him, you will miss what he wants to do. Don't miss it—obey God and follow the Holy Spirit. Make up in your mind to not miss God. When you are clear, your elevation is near. Here are some keys to keeping yourself in position.

1. Commit to Jesus. No more wishy-washy ups and downs, no more cheating on him with other idols, beliefs, or ideologies. There is one person you will report to and get your direction from from now on.

2. Consecrate yourself. The Lord will not bless a mess. He cannot and will not condone or make exceptions for sin! Take your consecration seriously, and watch the Lord do amazing things in your life.

3. Get your house in order. The Lord cannot release certain blessings to those who are unorganized, scattered, double-minded, or out of order. Prepare to be blessed by getting your house in order. Tie up loose ends, finish old projects, plan to address old debts, and show the Lord you are taking the initiative, are responsible, and are a good steward.

4. Live well. Get out of the world. You cannot have one foot on holy ground and the other foot in a mud puddle. Sooner or later, you'll get muddy. Jesus is calling you to clean living in every way—thoughts, associations, diet, and how you live in general. It's time to live worthy of the blessings you seek.

5. Let Jesus lead. He knows how to get you to where you need to be, he knows how to open doors, he knows where you need to go, and he knows how to get you there, so commit to letting the Lord lead. In this season, you will let God order your steps, and you will make great and rapid progress.

The Lord frequently has reminded me that he is working more behind the scenes of my life than I can see. He is working more things out for me when I rest in him than I could ever imagine or accomplish on my own. The Lord spoke to me one day: *I can do more for you with you in the prayer room for one hour than if you worked a hundred hours behind the desk on a project.* One word from God changes everything. The Lord wants you to focus on pursuing intimacy with him.

Prayer gives you access to more than you realize. It's not just about taking your petitions to the throne though you should and you must. It's also about personal communion with God, because you need him and what only he can give; you need the benefits of regular communion with you Father.

Jesus routinely got up early to pray alone. Notice the powerful progression and revelation in Mark.

> Very early in the morning, while it was still dark, Jesus got up, left the house and went off to a solitary place, where he prayed. Simon and his companions went to look for him, and when they found him, they exclaimed: "Everyone is looking for you!" Jesus replied, "Let us go somewhere else—to the nearby villages—so I can preach there also. That is why I have come." So he traveled throughout Galilee, preaching in their synagogues and driving out demons. (Mark 1:35–39 NLT)

Jesus prayed alone and emerged energized, clear, focused, and driven regarding his destiny.

- The key to your clarity is prayer.
- The key to your assignment is prayer.

- The key to your elevation will come because of instructions given to you in prayer.
- Your peace will come in prayer.
- Your directions will come in prayer.
- Your breakthrough will come in prayer.

Now that the prayer part is clear, here are some key verses about how to get it right.

> But when you pray, go into your room, close the door and pray to your Father, who is unseen. Then your Father, who sees what is done in secret, will reward you. (Matt. 6:6 NIV)

> Very early in the morning, while it was still dark, Jesus got up, left the house and went off to a solitary place, where he prayed. (Mark 1:35 NIV)

> The effectual fervent prayer of a righteous man availeth much. (James 5:16 NIV)

When you decree and declare these in Jesus's name, your prayers will not return void. To gain strength, greater alignment with God, and clarity regarding your destiny, pray fervently and regularly. This seemingly simple revelation is powerful because the Father is telling you not to focus on your calling or destiny. Instead, you must remain fully focused on him, and he will lead you to his plan for you. Matthew 6 reads, "But seek first the kingdom of God and his righteousness, and all these things shall be added to you" (Matt. 6:33 KJV). God has in mind everything you need; he has that covered and is in control.

There is freedom when you say yes to the kingdom of God. Being elevated to his kingdom is not about rules, regulations, or systems but about a relationship with him. When you say yes to the kingdom of God, you are saying yes to a life of freedom. God's kingdom is mentioned over 160 times in the New Testament, and every time, it talks about how God longs to see his kingdom manifested on earth. He manifests his kingdom on earth through his sons and daughters who have said yes. Faith is increased when you say yes to his kingdom; God will use your yes to grow your faith.

You are about to walk in God's identity with his authority and see his power. In this past season, God placed many people where they learned to understand their true identities hidden in God. When the Lord finds people who seek him at a deeper level, he gives them full authority and access to his power. We are about to enter a 2 Chronicles 16:9 season. The eyes of the Lord are running to and fro throughout the whole earth searching for those whose hearts are loyal to him so he can show himself strong on their behalf.

The reason you went through everything you did in the past season was to benefit you for the promotion God has for you in this season. It was necessary for you to not just go through that season but also grow through that season.

God has no limits, so you never have to settle for dreaming small. You will have to disconnect from many people before you can step into your next season. You will have to renew your mind-set and think on a higher level. Poverty mind-sets will not be allowed to follow you into your next season.

Many times, you think you have an option to obey what the Lord has said to do or not. God drops dreams, destinies, purposes, and ideas in your spirit because he wants to see it accomplished on earth. When you receive an assignment or purpose from God, he is trusting you to help carry out a significant part of his plan. When you are caught up in the prophetic flow God has for your life, he will cause you to jump in the middle of his will. The Lord is saying, "Jump off of the bank and jump into the river of God!" When you completely jump into the river of God, you will go with the flow of his will and kingdom. Allow the Lord to do what he needs to do in your life and just flow with him.

Every prophetic word and promise you have from God is a seed. When Satan hears a prophetic word that a man or woman of God released over you, he immediately starts trying to abort that seed. But remember, "'No weapon forged against you will prevail, and you will refute every tongue that accuses you. This is the heritage of the servants of the LORD, and this is their vindication from me,' declares the LORD" (Isa. 54:17 NIV). The devil will try to use all his wiles to try to stop the word God planted in you. Satan never goes to war where there are no spoils.

Once you step out and start walking out the prophetic words God has spoken over your life, you begin an incredible, life-altering journey with him. When you step out, you step up into a new season of your life. God is raising and elevating new people to higher levels of business and ministry.

If you've heard the Lord say he would swing the doors wide open, he will do so even when that seems impossible, and he will do it in such a grand fashion that you'll be able to run through those doors at full speed.

Don't look at where you are; look at where you're going. Make sure you're connected to the right people in this season. Surround yourself with only those who will help you walk in the purposes and plans God has over your life. In Hebrews, Paul said, "We do not want you to become lazy, but to imitate those who through faith and patience inherit what has been promised" (Heb. 6:12 NIV).

The hour we are in is a special time for the body of Christ; make sure that those around you are spiritually strong. Grow close to those who have been through hard times and followed God all the way through until they got their breakthroughs. Align yourself with people who stay in the battle until they inherit the promises and the purpose God has designed for them.

PROMPT FOR REFLECTION

Is it your time for elevation? Are you in position?

PRAYER

Lord, help me to keep my eyes looking straight ahead and not back on the former days and old ways of doing things. I know you want to do something new in my life. Help me concentrate on where I am going to go now, not where I have been. Release me from the past so I can move out of it and into the future you have for me.

Conclusion

And we boast in the hope of the glory of God.
—Romans 5:2 NIV

Sometimes, we can be our own worst setbacks. As his children, God gives us command of our situations. We are no longer just human beings after we are born again; we become spirit beings in human form to perform great exploits. Keeping God at the center of our lives will help us become conscious of our supernatural status and enjoy his glory.

The highest level of faith is resting in God. Faith comes before understanding. If God's ways were small enough for you to understand, he wouldn't be big enough for you to entrust your life to. Hope is an intensive expectancy of the glory. Get in his atmosphere of glory and watch for greater miracles. It's not yesterday's anointing you want but today's anointing and God's glory, which are available right now. His glory is his presence, but unbelief can deny you that.

You have to have a connection and a relationship with God because you are constantly in movement and otherwise would have no idea where you are. Scripture accurately speaks to where you are. When you are in the wilderness, don't believe its bad rep; no wilderness means no Promised Land. The wilderness has purpose; character is built there, your drama is healed in the wilderness, you discover God there, and you find yourself there. Get to the place where you can say, "God, I don't want the Promised Land until you work out everything that needs to be worked out of me." Be more concerned about who you are becoming than where you are going. You were created in the image of God; that means you're somebody, and the wilderness is the only place where your becoming unfolds.

That's why David said create within me a pure heart and renew a right spirit within me. He didn't want to be a carnal being; he wanted to be what people couldn't see—his spirit, the real him. The wilderness is the space between seasons, between what was and what will be. You can be comfortable in Egypt until God shakes things up, turns up the heat, and makes you uncomfortable to the point that you cry out.

Doubters can see potential, but the difference between a believer and a doubter is that a believer goes after it. What is God showing you? What has he spoken to you? Was it a promise you treated only as potential? It is so if you go after it. Maybe leaves room for alternative narratives, and all Satan needs is a crack to get you to start doubting the promise.

It isn't until you see the promise in the potential that you move into what God has for you. It's not a maybe; it's going to happen just the way God said it would. It'll start with what you see and what you call it. It will change your approach and how you go after it. It's all in how you allow yourself to see it. Those who see correctly go in and lay hold of everything God promised. If you leave the door open, you'll run back to the place God delivered you from because you're so faithless and doubt is deadly; you can't play with it because it's after the promise.

The Word of God is the raw material you need mixed with faith to profit you. He gives you the raw materials that you bring your belief to. It's not a game. You can ask things of the test. Caleb was led into the Promised Land because he had a spirit of faith: "But because my servant Caleb has a different spirit and follows me wholeheartedly, I will bring him into the land he went to, and his descendants will inherit it" (Num. 14:24 NIV). From this, you can see that doubt has an atmosphere but so does faith. It is a posture, a perspective, a declaration. Which one are you? If it's doubt, clear the air of that doubt.

Caleb's spirit gave him the power to hush the environment around him. If you're going to walk out the call of God on your life and be everything God has called you to be, you'll have to operate and flow in the Spirit because the enemy will always make sure you have an adequate amount of opposing opinions around and in you.

Learn how to allow the Holy Spirit to change your spirit as foreign things enter your life and negative things come into your mind. If you don't know how to hush those voices, you'll never produce the environment the promises are meant to grow in. Sometimes to create that environment, you'll have to leave an environment.

Refuse to tolerate noise so you can hear God. When the wrong thoughts come, hush them so they don't take root in your feelings and affect your emotions and beliefs to the point that they gain a stronghold. You have to release yourself from the need and forgive yourself because if you don't, you'll be charging and firing up the wrong atmosphere. The you who did the wrong things no longer exists. Drop the foolishness and remain present with the wise you. You have a Savior who took all your sin and remembers it no more, so neither should you carry it around any longer. Let your spirit mature.

The spirit of calm, of peace, of hush is your weapon against all the negatives in your life. Spiritual maturity is getting to a place where you can change your environment. How clear the promises would be if you could silence the other narratives. How much strength you would regain if you operated in the Holy Spirit, focused only on every situation that worked, and did not distrust voices. It's better to believe the best and be wrong than to believe the worst and be wrong. Don't rob yourself of a blessing God sends your way. When you're tempted to think negative, ask for the grace to see differently.

Often what you see as failure is what God's about to speed up in your life. He's positioning you to catch you up and do what you didn't know you could or needed to do. If you don't abort the mission, God will blow your mind. Don't ever allow yourself to get back to your hostage situation. Allow God to keep you out of your own way. Ask him to expose the places you need to take care of so he can take you to the places you need to go.

When you are down to nothing, you have to learn to speak to yourself to cause a paradigm shift. Speaking the truth, prophesying the Word of God, is the best thing you can do. Here are some subtle shifts to bring you back.

1. Practice thinking better about yourself. Sometimes, a loss in your life is an answered prayer, so stop belittling yourself. See yourself as worthy and lovable so you stop betraying yourself and become whole. When you don't know who God is, you look horizontally on social media, devalue yourself, and lose your purpose trying to fit in. Do things for the right reasons; God is trusting you to allow your soul to be built up because when he turns the light on, you better be ready. Refuse to belittle yourself; quote scripture until you believe it.

2. Embrace the fact that you are more than the one broken piece of yourself. Get yourself back to the basics; the only way the enemy can get you is by putting you somewhere that you feel unworthy to be. He tries to get you to think you're not who you really are. When God opens major doors for you, you'll come under attack, so realize that when the enemy starts fighting you, something major is about to happen in your life.

3. Change, evolve, and start over when you must. You can't get off the path. God loves to show out, so get where you need to be and allow God to do what he does even if you're not sure of it; it's still a part of your growth. There is no failure with God; keep moving and the door will open. It's okay to make U-turns and admit and celebrate mistakes. God knows what is, but when we carry loads we're not supposed to carry, we can't hear God, who is waiting on us.

4. Let go of what you don't need. God has created you for new things, so don't compromise and make trade-offs. Make the best of every outcome; you will get a lot of what you want if you manage your time, resources, and attitude. What you need is always more of God, so pray and refuse to fight the battle yourself.

5. Accept and embrace daily discomfort for the right reason. God is trying to give you the world, so position yourself for that and don't get caught up in things that won't enhance you. Nothing great is ever achieved in your comfort zone; discomfort caused us to grow into our most blessed and confident selves. Be intentional about getting to know the Father's heart and allow him to

recalibrate you. Lay hands on yourself; you don't have to know what you're doing—just be willing and trust him; don't lie down and remain a victim in your own story. Praise your way through, and live your best day today. Equip yourself with the life tools found in the Word.

6. Be mindful daily. Be aware of the present without wishing it were different. Find something to be grateful in the present moment. Let God fix your heart so you release and connect properly. The joy of the Lord shouldn't come and go with your circumstances.

7. Help someone else.

8. Open your hands and run into your future—he is your purpose.

God can do great things in the lives of those who are sold out to him. You can see this in the relationship between Joshua and God. Out of nowhere, the people of Gibeon came to Joshua's camp because they'd heard about his God.

> Your servants have come from a very distant country because of the fame of the Lord your God. For we have heard reports of him: all that he did in Egypt, and all that he did to the two kings of the Amorites east of the Jordan—Sihon king of Heshbon, and Og king of Bashan, who reigned in Ashtaroth. And our elders and all those living in our country said to us, "Take provisions for your journey; go and meet them and say to them, 'We are your servants; make a treaty with us.'" (Josh. 9:9–11 NLT)

No matter how much faith you have or how many times you've seen God show up for you, it is not a good day when all your enemies roll up on you. When they come against you, when this comes against you, when that falls apart, when this relationship dies or that financial difficulty arises, you'll feel attacked on every side just when you thought you were on the brink of your blessing.

You think that because of all the prophetic words you heard, you were going to the next dimension and it would be your time, but you look around and all hell breaks out and your enemies prosper. What do you do in seasons when it seems trouble is greater than blessings? Trouble doesn't come when you're ready to break through; trouble comes when you've broken through. You are in the Promised Land but don't realize it. Everything looks like difficulty, struggle, and war because you're in the enemy's camp.

You may think you're in the wilderness when you're really in the Promised Land. You're in the space of the promise; you don't need a breakthrough because you've already broken through, and that's why it's so difficult. You don't call for help for something that isn't greater than you.

Recognize where and who you are because if you don't know who you are, people will take advantage of you and cause you to miss your opportunities. When you step into it, you have to recognize the weight of who you are and resist the voices that try to make you believe you are less than who you are. Know that you are valuable. Refuse to make decisions that if you knew who you were you wouldn't make. Remember who you are.

What allows you to walk in your Promised Land is what you worked out in your wilderness. Get to a place where you are determined; assume the stance even if it costs you everything. You can be like everyone else and take the scraps thrown at you, murmur, complain, and walk in fear, or you can have a different spirit and believe in and trust God. Belief or unbelief—the black or white that will take you through the grey. Be hot or cold, not lukewarm—either you're in or you're not; you can't pretend with faith. God knows your heart, and the call on your life demands it. You have to see yourself right.

When you don't realize you've already broken through, you neglect to tighten things up. Things have to be tighter in the Promised Land than they were in the wilderness. Every dimension God takes you to will necessitate a tightening of your team because the altitude has changed; so has the level of security and safety that requires. You can't fight new devils with old disciplines. If you don't tighten things up, you can be tricked. You have to watch and be on guard differently. Who are the Judases on this level? Learn how to function on this new level. Reclaiming your authority was only the first step. Walking like Joshua is a relationship that comes from commitment, faith, and belief.

The closer you get to your purpose, the more opposition you will face. But God will counter all the opposition, betrayal, and false accusations the enemy throws at you. Pray for your Judases and not be offended by them; rather, wash their feet. God will use what they meant to destroy you to propel you toward your purpose. Some people look for opportunities to betray you. Let them. They will talk, plan, scheme, and lie to try to come against you. Let them. God will use them to help you arrive at your purpose.

The enemy wants to stop your purpose. He will try to use those closest to you. Jesus trusted Judas to handle his finances, but Judas betrayed him. Don't be offended by your betrayers because God will use them to lead you to your destiny. Jesus called Judas a friend because Jesus knew Judas's betrayal would lead him closer to his destiny. The enemy will try to use your family and friends to discourage you from pursuing your purpose. So many people's destinies have been stopped by close friends, parents, and family members.

When Joshua was in a difficult situation, he was unstoppable, and so are you. Don't be distracted by what comes against you; learn what it communicates to you. You have broken through, so see yourself there, tighten things up, and keep walking. Don't decrease your prayer life. God will be with you and back you up.

It takes courage to be unique. We don't hear that often. We resist reformation and transformation; we run from it for excitement and praising. If our lives will change, we can't remain the same. Acts says, "Repent, then, and turn to God, so that your sins may be wiped out, that times of refreshing may come from the Lord" (Acts 3:19 NIV). Repenting is turning from whatever keeps us from God. When we know God has more for us, our response should change so we can be ready to receive it.

Change how you walk with him, pray for it, work for it, labor for it, give up for it, and turn down opportunities because the kingdom of heaven is at hand. How many things will you change to get it? The people you would think would be the most receptive of you may reject you. Be willing to sacrifice to lay hold of the promise. God won't pull you out of the foolishness you're enjoying; you must repent or miss out.

You don't really have a ministry until you're challenged. The cost of being used by God is being hated; that's being like Jesus. Isn't it funny that we say one thing until it happens? When there is nothing to complain about, are you happy or addicted to dysfunction? Opposition is part of the process; it helps you know who you are. You don't really know who you are until people oppose you. Will you say yes to God and obey him? Will you say the right things but not do them? Repenting and following him means doing the Father's will. When the Father comes to you, what will you do?

When you stare at a message, it gets bigger; you see what it deals with and how it applies to your life. If you call yourself a child of God, you ought to be willing to do what's asked because he's given you enough. God's already invested in you; he ought to be able to send you, and you ought to be able to go. If you don't have a love that allows people to grow, you don't know what love is; love always for change. God is waiting on you. He wants you back. Help him help you turn around.

Your mind tends to believe whatever it is fed, so feed it well. Feed it faith. Feed it truth. Feed it love. Be so strong in the Lord and Jesus that you're too hot for the enemy to handle and negative people won't want to be near you.

That podcast? Launch it.
That blog? Start it.
That book? Write it.
That idea? Flesh it out.
That app? Develop it.
That gift? Put it to use.
The impossible? Achieve it.
This time it will be different.

What King has rule of your life? Focus on the one who came to save, the great problem solver. You are a royal priesthood; make sure your walk matches that. God is backing you, so nothing can prevail against you. Never take God for granted; always give him the glory. To God be the glory!

A LITTLE SOMETHING EXTRA

Ten Things to Work to Keep You Walking Worthily

1. Meditate on the Word of God versus reflecting on issues.
2. Be an empty vessel so God can fill you. What is most important to keep an inventory of?
3. Keep studying the Bible definition of what love is and apply it to yourself.
4. Keep dying to yourself—release what you want and the way you think things should or you'll miss what is.
5. Guard what you come into agreement with.
6. Refuse to accept and open gifts from the enemy.
7. Keep your coaching sessions with God.
8. Release self-effort and take greater risks of faith.
9. Rest in God. Rest equals trust, faith, and alignment in him.
10. Share your testimony.

CPSIA information can be obtained
at www.ICGtesting.com
Printed in the USA
BVHW03*0954030718
520736BV00003B/7/P

9 781982 206499